THE DEVELOPMENT AND ANTIDEVELOPMENT DEBATE

T0347469

To my father (in memoriam) and to my mother
for the hopes that they instilled.

To Clara, Adib and Duda
for the promises that they hold.

The Development and Antidevelopment Debate

Critical Reflections on the Philosophical Foundations

MARTHA JALALI RABBANI
Kansas University, USA

Routledge
Taylor & Francis Group

LONDON AND NEW YORK

First published 2011 by Ashgate Publishing

2 Park Square, Milton Park, Abingdon, Oxon OX14 4RN
711 Third Avenue, New York, NY 10017, USA

Routledge is an imprint of the Taylor & Francis Group, an informa business

First issued in paperback 2016

British Library Cataloguing in Publication Data
Jalali Rabbani, Martha.
  The development and antidevelopment debate : critical reflections on the
  philosophical foundations.
  1. Economic development—Social aspects. 2. Economic assistance—Social aspects.
  3. Dependency. 4. Autonomy (Philosophy)
  I. Title
  306.3–dc22

Library of Congress Control Number: 2011920502

ISBN 978-1-4094-0997-7 (hbk)
ISBN 978-1-138-26093-1 (pbk)

Contents

Preface

The ongoing debate between the advocates of development and its critics has been built mainly on an antagonism established in modern times between the preservation of individual rights, on the one hand, and those of the community, on the other. The debate over development has, moreover, reinforced this modern antagonism by altogether shunning away from an open reflection on the normative conditions of practical relations or by taking for granted the antagonistic and non-reconciliatory structure of the normativity set forth by the modern discourse.

The normative conditions of social relations can be explained in terms of peoples' interdependency at the level of their self-relation. Without an acknowledgement of the reconciliatory structure of this interdependency, I want to argue, proposals for social change, either in the direction of global development or communities' right to self-determination, are doomed to repeat the same oppositional power relations, substituting at best one social group or one set of social boundaries by another. As the condition of possibility of coexistence, people's inalienable interdependency is to be made evident and understood before prevailing patterns of interaction can be criticized and alternative ones legitimized and re-ordered.

In an effort to contribute with the enduring inquiry into the legitimacy of development's project, this book examines the philosophical foundations of the main disagreements that surround development discourse. I review the normative assumptions that are implied in the development debate to argue that, in spite of proclaimed divergences, the discourses of both sides, when looked at from a normative perspective, are very similar to each other. Antidevelopmentists, thereof, offer no argument able to delegitimize the project of development and no real alternatives to the established order.

The power structure that development legitimizes remains disturbingly unchallenged. Antidevelopment discourse, though many times effective in carrying on its social and political goals within communities, has not challenged development's power in its core assumptions. If the power relations that development justifies are, as antidevelopmentists alert us, oppressive, we need more than an alternative set of political actions or political rulers. Unless the way development describes and shapes social reality is normatively challenged, critics of development will continue to unintentionally support rather than weaken the *status quo*.

In the following pages, I argue that awareness of the condition of human unity or people's interdependency at the level of their search for self-understanding can demand respect to the rights of both individuals *and* communities to decide about the *good life*. I argue, moreover, that respect to these common rights, as long as it intends to attend to the search for self-understanding, does not imply freedom from the other's interference. Contrary to established assumptions in the development debate and in Modernity' discourse in general, respect to the equal right of individuals and communities implies, in principle, the *universal* validation of individual and group decisions.

From a normative standpoint, a decision-making process that potentially includes all human beings cannot be explained in terms of globalization alone, nor due to the threats that globalization may pose to survival. If survival was the main purpose, respect for the life of human beings could only be demanded to the extent that it is demanded for every other living creature. Furthermore, the inclusiveness of a decision-making process determined by the requirements of survival are conditional and self-defeating - as current international relations based on strategies of balance of power, economic gain or financial aid give witness to.

In contrast to the current patterns of social inclusion, the inclusion founded on the recognition of human unity or the interdependency of *all* peoples and individuals cannot exclude any one person or collectivity from the validation of the other's choices. Development policies conceived according to these lines can alone accomplish the practical goals of development and antidevelopment discourses respectively, namely the unfolding of individuals and community's unique and socially relevant qualities and capacities. Similarly, the recognition of human unity in their search for self-understanding demands respect to the other not in terms of everyone's right to decide on their own, but in terms of the *equal and irreplaceable value that everyone holds in giving meaning to everyone else's choices*.

Freedom as self-understanding requires the possibility of having one's choices universally validated. Contrary to what development has represented to the so called "underdeveloped", bilateral participation in decision-making processes, even in those traditionally regarded as private matters or issues of national security, should be the norm. Because people depend on each other for the fulfillment of their *search* for self-understanding, authentic development is only achieved, in the south but also in the north, in the east and in the west, when everyone is given an equal voice in decision-making processes that, in their turn, can only in this way become expressive of everyone's freedom.

From this perspective on development and freedom, it is without purpose to classify the peoples of the world as developed or underdeveloped. It would be more coherent to say, even with the goals of development project itself, that we currently live in an underdeveloped world which, in spite of differences in the material conditions of existence, is far from increasing its inhabitants' understanding of the value and meaning of their choices. People today in small or large communities, in traditional or liberal ones, long for social symbols and imitate established patterns of behavior for almost no other reason than to guarantee social recognition and to *preserve*, rather than to understand and fulfill, their individual and collective selves.

What I argue in this book is that development, understood as respect to and promotion of the diversity of individual and community life, can only be achieved when people restitute the struggle for self-preservation to its original place: at the service of self-understanding. The search for self-understanding for a humanity that cannot avoid its unity, and thus has of necessity to engage together in this search, is the legitimizing grounds for the modern moral claim that the diversity of human life *should* be respected and the practical possibility for the universal hope that it will eventually come to be so.

Martha Rabbani, October 2010

Acknowledgments

I am greatly in debt to the committed students and colleagues that I have worked with and to the generous and hopeful people that I have encountered throughout my community building efforts, whom defied every solid modern categorization. They were fundamental in shaping the ideas and arguments set forth here. The eventual materialization of this book I owe to the unconditional support and loving patience of my husband.

PART I
Grounding the Development Debate

Introduction to Part I

While development theory and practice has been the object of extensive study by critics and supporters alike, the analysis of the unspoken similarities between the discourses that stand for development, on the one hand, and those that oppose it, on the other, has for the most part been ignored or deemed unnecessary. If the debate over the desirability of modern forms of development intends, however, to go beyond the polarization of discourses and effectively contribute to the much anticipated social change that both sides foresee, such comparative approach is crucially needed.

The tools necessary to pursue this critical analysis are not likely to be found in the field of development studies itself, as it largely overlooks the normative structure of its own discourse.[1] These tools are widely available, however, in the discussions carried out in modern philosophy. These discussions, when revised and applied to the study of development and antidevelopment discourses, have the potential to rescue the debate from its tantalizing disagreements. They can simultaneously reveal the similarities in the hidden assumptions of both positions and re-evaluate their theoretical and practical shortcomings.

In order to pursue these two interdependent goals, I start with a particular argument from *Critical Theory* that, though well-established in modern political philosophy, has not yet been brought into the study of the development debate.[2] Initially systematized by two renowned and ground-breaking philosophers, Jurgen Habermas (1984) and Karl-Otto Apel (1984), the argument refers to the conditions of possibility of human understanding, in general, and to its characteristics as reflected in the structure of human communication, in specific. Its general tenet is that human communication, including development and antidevelopment discourses, is understandable because it is built on the assumption that the claims that are raised in speech can be universally validated, that is, because people communicate as if their claims were redeemable.[3]

---

1   Few exceptions to this norm would be the systematic normative approaches of Illich (1980), Sachs (1992) and Escobar (1995).

2   Critical Theory has, however, been a very important tool in the analysis of social discourses and practical politics in general. For the interested reader a good place to start would be Honneth, et al. (1997), originally published in commemoration of Habermas' sixtieth birthday.

3   In Communicative Theory the intelligibility of speech refers simultaneously to the redemption of the truth, sincerity and the normative correctness of the claims raised in speech. These claims refer respectively to the objective reality of measurable facts, to the inner and subjective world of the communicative agent and to the pre-established and

This philosophical argument has at least two important implications for the development debate. First, comparing the goals of development and antidevelopment discourses would require that the truth claims implicit in each side's discourse be seriously considered and sought after. Second, the *legitimization* of both sides' *power* claims would be placed within the context of these claims. In other words, the social value of the policies and proposals carried by each side would be critically assessed as their claims to the truth were identified, their validity questioned and the possibility of their redemption considered.

These two implications represent together to the development debate a reversal in the ongoing effort of social sciences, since the beginnings of Modernity, to lay bare the power relations hidden behind alleged claims to the truth.[4] As these sciences proclaim the alleged truth can be in fact an illusion. But it is not so only because it serves as a façade to the will to power. Behind a corrupt will to power lies yet an even more concealed possibility, one that sustains both power and the supposedly self-evident truths that it serves.

I will delve in a moment into this possibility and the "truth claims" raised in human communication. Before, however, I must acknowledge that social critique carried in terms of "truth" poses at best some risks, especially in the context of modern liberal societies. The most accepted way out of the difficulties that attachment to "truth" creates has been a general discursive and practical openness towards the diversity of existing positions and the institutionalization of a legal regulatory system that validates itself on the grounds of the equality of treatment that if confers to all. History, social critics argue, has repeatedly offered its testimony, always too late, to the cruelty of beliefs, which though later on proved otherwise, were at their own time accepted or imposed as unavoidable truths.

Social critique in modern times, including the critique of the debate over development, would seem to be better served by the language of "value". Values are defined as social constructs determined by the material and/or symbolic conditions of each society. Unlike truth, the language of value offers in itself no criteria for comparing or evaluating different value systems.[5]

A "value oriented" approach to reality represents supposedly both practical and normative advantages in relation to a "truth oriented" approach. Practically speaking, it can ease social tensions by making differences look less threatening. Each person or culture is to be respected (or at least tolerated) in its diversity because differences do not detract or add to the beholders worth. As long as

---

pre-agreed world of social norms. Here I will be referring to all these claims in a non-differentiated manner, as "truth claims". See Habermas (1984) for an in-depth analysis of Communicative Theory.

4   See Habermas (1990b) for a comprehensive analysis of this philosophical and historical trend.

5   Sandel (2010) sums up most compelling arguments in his recent analysis of the claimed social benefits and the downside of liberals' "aspiration to neutrality".

differences simply reflect contingent social constructs or inventions, exclusions cannot be justified, at least not on these grounds.

Normatively speaking, the language of value gives unaccounted recognition to human equality. When applied to the critique of development, for instance, the classification of peoples as developed or underdeveloped, as antidevelopmentists remind us, becomes meaningless. A social construct, "development" cannot place some in a position of superiority in relation to others. Because people are equal in their capacity to choose their values, relationships should always be on the basis of mutual respect and tolerance.

The role of social critique has been, in general terms, to determine criteria to denounce patterns of social exclusion and legitimize social inclusion. This means that social critique is concerned with instances of social injustice or oppression. The value approach to reality has promised critical theorists a means to name and identify social oppression without legitimizing, in the process, new forms of exclusion or intolerance. Nothing could pose less risk and thus be more attractive than such a promise to those committed with the project of a more equitable society. It is as attractive, however, as the possibility of eating one's cake and keeping it at the same time.

Within this context, what would be the benefits of thinking about the development debate asking first about the truth claims implied in it? Why is that identifying the truth claims underneath the discourse would be more effective in delegitimizing development's power rather than invalidating the possibility of truth itself? I have here no ambition or expertise to quench the epistemological thirst that statements on truth may give rise to. But some conceptual clarifications are in fact needed before I can continue with my analysis of the development debate.

Following the tradition of *Universal Pragmatics* laid out by Jurgen Habermas and Karl-Otto Apel, I refer to "truth" as that unconditional structure of daily action and interaction, and which these authors refer to as the *condition of possibility* of human action in society. *Universal Pragmatics* is particularly concerned with determining the conditions of possibility of intelligible communication between human beings. In general terms, communication is understandable because whosoever communicates makes claims that, though raised in a particular context, have a presumption of universal validity.[6] In other words, the interlocutors accept, either voluntarily or involuntarily, that the claims that they raise in communication can be redeemed, if and should their validity be questioned, by anyone and at any time – and thus the possibility of understanding and agreement.

We infer from the above that truth refers foremost to a "moment of *unconditionality*" built into the structure of human action. Human beings may choose not to act in a particular way, such as communicate in an understandable way. In case they do choose so, however, they succeed in their purpose because of this moment or universal structure that is already in place and regulates their interactions.

---

6   See Habermas (1990a).

In Habermas' Communicative Theory, "truth" refers to one particular aspect of that unconditional structure that constitutes human action: the *presumption* of universal agreement built into the expectations of those who communicate. "Truth" exists, therefore, because, as Apel and Habermas have explained, regardless of whether we can all agree or not on what the truth is – or on what these basic universal structures would be – we all communicate with each other, in fact can *only* do so, *as if* such universal agreement was possible.

Mutual agreement is simultaneously sought, either openly or implicitly, in relation to three different spheres of validity: the objective world of facts, the subjective reality of the individual speaker and the intersubjective realm of norms. Although not all these three spheres of truth claims are simultaneously questioned in daily communication, when they are questioned, it is the presumption of universal agreement that guarantees the possibility of mutual understanding.

When we apply these philosophers' effort to identify "what we must necessarily always already presuppose in regard to ourselves and others as normative conditions of the possibility of understanding; and in this sense what we must necessarily always already have accepted"[7] to the study of the development debate, we can move the debate forward both at the discursive level and in terms of its practical applications.

Contrary to what a value oriented tradition in social critique would argue, the *possibility* of universal agreement on the conditions that have "always already" been accepted by everyone and also on new realities that may be created, binds people together in a *non-contingent* and *normative* solidarity. In fact, while a value approach to reality can at best promote a causal solidarity – in the case that two or more collectivities share the same belief system – the recognition of the universal structure of human interaction in terms of redeemable claims thrive on an inalienable search for mutual agreement. The one who raises a claim always expects to be understood and, in the case that someone cares to understand him, this claim will be more or less challenged and, accordingly, eventually validated or replaced by a better, truer or more truthful claim.

Truth claims thus, by their very nature, bind people in their communicative capacity together determining thus a universal interdependency with important implications for the relationship between cultures and societies. Societies are internally ordered and stable because they have managed to establish a level of agreement reflected in a particular political culture. At the same time, each society would most likely disagree with some or many aspects of the others' political culture. This factual external disagreement implies that to keep a legitimate internal order, societies have to redeem their claims, externally but mainly internally – to its own members who will be the most directly affected by these claims and thus the most interested in questioning their validity – in face of external demands for justification.

---

7   Karl-Otto Apel in Outhwaite (1996): 118.

The demand for intercultural and international accountability as a requirement for an internal order that is built on just terms, that is answerable to the questioning of its own members, signifies an important change to the way development is conceptualized, criticized and implemented. In a value oriented discourse, neither internal nor international solidarity can be justified in a normative or non-contingent way. As independent actors, individuals or societies can expect equal respect only as long as they are capable of creating an effective balance of educational, economic or military power. The social problem that both sides in the development debate have tried to address, namely the terms of a fair cooperation among the members of society and between the peoples of the world, is thus submitted to the practical realm of efficient power display.

I will next make an initial introduction to the normative structure of human relations and develop this reflection further in the third part, as I explain the terms of a fair relationship between the peoples of the world and redefine development. In this first introductory part three points have to be addressed in the context of the development debate: 1) the claims that are raised in the development and antidevelopment discourses and their condition of possibility; 2) the meaning and implications of this condition for social action and 3) the similar ways in which the types of action or the claims to power that both discourses legitimize fall short from their intended goals, a discussion which will be deepened in the second part of this book.

Chapter 1
The Debate and its Claims: Oppression, Value and Poverty

Antidevelopment and development discourses are built on widely known claims that shape and give meaning to their mutual disagreements. Although disagreements revolve around a variety of different issues, the words oppression, value construction and poverty are a required presence in all of them.

At first glance it may seem that the sides are making opposite claims on these central issues but an analysis of the less evident requirements and implications of these claims, followed by a reflection on the conditions of possibility of oppression, values and poverty, reveals important and fundamental similarities. Ignoring the condition of possibility of its own concealed claims, the debate over development simultaneously a) gives the false impression that development and antidevelopment goals substantially differ from each other and that each, thereof, represent a real alternative to the established social order and b) overlooks and delegitimizes the very requirements for a reasonable estimation of the social desirability of their goals.

On Oppression and Freedom

To identify the unspoken requirements and implications of the claims raised in the development debate, let us first start in the way that any antidevelopmentist would, with the language of oppression. Critique to modern development is built on the original assumption that different life styles hold an equal right to exist, that is, hold an essential equal value and that this right is being denied through the spread of development. Development is oppressive because it denies to people and their cultures this equality.

On a more attentive look, however, the language of oppression implies more than the equality of the oppressed and oppressor's choices. It also implies that the oppressed and oppressor are of a certain constituency. In fact, we can only explain and understand oppression because a judgment has already been passed on the quality of the parties involved. In describing, for instance, how two inert objects are placed on top of each other, one would hardly make sense of an explanation that referred to it as oppressive. Not every act of destruction, therefore, no matter how devastating, is oppressive.

Whether the oppressor or oppressed are aware of it or not – and whether antidevelopmentists agree with it or not – denouncing oppression is only possible under the condition of an inalienable freedom. Freedom as the capacity to choose one's way of life, without the other's interference, is what gives rise to oppression. It is people's equality in this particular condition that allows us to understand the word "oppression". Without freedom we would be subject to death, destruction or disintegration but not oppression. Naming oppression is, before anything else, the recognition that some have been deprived of their inalienable capacity to choose and the demand that others take responsibility for their free choice to oppress.

It is important to clarify that although the assumption of the non-conditionality of freedom is at the center of a discourse on oppression, this assumption represents a particular cultural and historical valorization of freedom. Antidevelopmentists expect to make a *compelling* case against the modern project of development when explaining it in terms of "oppression" because their audience, like themselves and everyone else, lives in a special time, a time that understands and values the claims of freedom.

By denouncing development as oppressive, antidevelopmentists are saying that development project did not acknowledge and valued what everyone else can reasonably appreciate in modern times, namely the non-conditionality of freedom. Though many would argue that developmentists and antidevelopmentists subscribe to different notions of freedom, the modernity of both discourses comes to surface when the practical requirement and implication of freedom in each one of these discourses is analyzed.

It is well-established that while antidevelopment discourse values freedom in terms of community's right to self-determination, developmentists value individual freedom in the liberal sense of the word.[1] These two apparently opposite definitions, however, have a common requirement: non-interference in the domain of the other. Because of it, we can say that freedom for both liberals and communitarians, developmentists and antidevelopmentists alike, has the same negative meaning: freedom *from* the interference of others in one's individual or community choices.

From this common basis on negative freedom, development and antidevelopment discourses converge in another important aspect. Because negative freedom can only be claimed for agents capable of positive choice, both those who defend or attack development cannot make a claim for freedom without valuing, simultaneously, *positive* freedom.

---

1   The discussions that have been raised by authors like Taylor (1994), Nussbaum and Cohen (1996), Habermas (1998), Young (2000) and Benhabib (2006) around issues such as constitutional law, human rights and world citizenship in multicultural societies are an effort to reflect on the apparently unsurpassable gap between liberal and communitarian interpretations of freedom.

Just as the placement of one inert object on top of another cannot be reasonably referred to as an oppressive event, it would also be a stretch of imagination to try to set one of these objects *free*. In other words, negative freedom is meaningful when claimed for beings that are capable of exercising positive freedom: the freedom to choose and do things that one is capable of as a free agent. The content of this positive freedom, the choices that one will make should not, by definition, be predetermined. They can, in principle, be anything, from pursuing economical growth to deciding against it; from choosing to modernize or creating hybrid cultures[2] or yet remaining traditional.

Although positive freedom is stressed in one case as a community right and in the other as an individual right, for both development and antidevelopment approaches, freedom has the same implication, that is, serves one and the same purpose: the legitimization of the established order. From a modern, liberal and developmentist perspective, the individual can only make use of his or her personal freedom within a society that is carefully designed to maximize individual rational choice – expressed more likely than not in a capitalist economic order and through free market mechanisms – while protecting the same right for all its members. Freedom is thus open ended or undecided only for the individual but not for the society within which this individual functions. Ironically, the *sin qua non* condition of individual's freedom to "act as he or she pleases" is a social order that is already in place, independently of individual or group choices. This is why the so called liberal democracies try to sharply differentiate between the "private" and the "public" spheres of life, while seeking by all means to protect one against the interferences of the other.

In traditional societies, and more unequivocally in the discourse of antidevelopmentists, positive choice is primordially a collective right, regardless of how and what purpose freedom is exercised for. The implication of this claim is that the regulation of collective life should not be subject to external interference and not even necessarily answerable to internal demands. Like liberal societies, traditional ones do not contemplate in their internal organization a place for questioning established goals and structures. Unlike them, however, traditional orders are not *a priori* bind to justify themselves in any particular term, i.e. the maximization of individual freedom or self-interest.

Developmentists and antidevelopmentists, while apparently disagreeing on the meaning and the value of freedom, use the concept to legitimize a preferred order while delegitimizing choices that would threaten this order. No clear criteria exist in either discourse to question and validated the goals and the means of individual and collective freedom. In the absence of such criteria, the established order reigns supreme.

Although it is clear that freedom is a foundational claim in both development and antidevelopment discourses, making a variety of posterior claims understandable, it is not clear, however, how such an emptied concept can be of any practical value

---

2   See for instance Escobar (1995) for a definition of hybrid cultures.

to societies and individuals alike, how it can guide their lives or set any substantial goals. More than empowering them, it constrains them to the limits of the socially acceptable. "Freedom" so loosely defined can hardly be of any help to those who witness their capacity to choose systematically reaped off and replaced by the "rightful" choice *for* a free society.

On Value and Truth

In order to promote the right of communities to a free and equal coexistence in the international scenario, antidevelopmentists have revealed the oppressive nature of development by asserting the value of positive freedom at the community level. A central argument used to value freedom at this level has been that every human project, including the project of development, is a community or societal value construction, a contingent and historically bound reality, which cannot, therefore, be universally validated.[3]

This argument, although intended to foster negative freedom from development interventions and positive freedom for communities, cannot fulfill its intended goal. It creates in a sense a paradox. The more antidevelopmentists try to justify the requirement of mutual respect by evidencing the value-laden nature of the development project, the more they undermine this goal. Instead of a free and equal, that is, fair coexistence between societies, their discourse can only create resentment and suspicion. The coexistence that it fosters is among those who, helpless about the possibility of universal validation and mutual understanding, tolerate each other under constant mutual surveillance and imposed restraint.

Antidevelopmentists defend the right of communities to positive choice but only through a costly means. They overlook that claims raised by peoples and communities are also claims to the truth and that collective choices are not simply a contingent reality but have the pretension of universal validity. By overlooking this normative condition of positive freedom, antidevelopmentists undermine the meaning and the value of communities' choices. The meaning of a particular life style to those who subscribe to it lies precisely in the possibility of validating it beyond one's own community, to *anyone* who asks to be convinced of its value.

It was only in modern times – partly as a requirement of the expansion of multicultural societies and the establishment of Democratic Constitutional States, partly due to the development of mass communication which brought the world with its great diversity of traditions and life styles closer together and partly as a reaction against the global and arbitrary spread of the Enlightenment project – that the truth had to be tamed and contained within community borders. Nowadays even more traditional communities try to adapt their discourses to the new waves of post-modernism. It is important to remember, however, that when Native Americans, for instance, talked about mother-earth they were not talking about their piece of

3   Escobar 1995.

land being of value and having to be respected by them alone. They were talking about the *true* condition of the earth, that the earth is their mother and the mother of everyone else, including the white man's. That was so much the case that the consequences for disrespecting this condition would affect natives and whites alike. Mother-earth reacts in the same way with whosoever disrespects her.[4]

By changing the status of the development project to a value construction, antidevelopmentists stand in an ambiguous position, a place where any claim to the truth is undermined. Hence, in the process of defending communities and their claims to the truth, there is nothing fundamentally left to be defended. In order to promote a free and equal coexistence among communities, antidevelopmentists end up significantly altering and impoverishing the meaning of communities' choices and thus communities' self-relation. Under such circumstances the goal of an equal and free coexistence becomes as oppressive as development's interventions. Societies do not have the practical power to share their truths nor the means to legitimize such right, becoming thus the victims of indefinable oppression, that is, the victims of a reality that has not yet even been recognized or named as oppressive.

Antidevelopmentists, without concern for the truth claims that communities raise, argue that since everything is a matter of value, the development project should be kept within the confines of its own birthplace. The less evident implication of such claim is that everyone else should also do the same. This lack of awareness about the condition of possibility of a meaningful choice asks communities to lower their voices, silence their claims, if they are to expect equal treatment in the international scenario. Far from fostering respect to and nurturing the diversity of life styles, this argument depicts a world that welcomes only those who abide by the limited place they have been assigned to, either by the restricting power of the enemy or by their well-intended representatives.

The abyss between the antidevelopmentist's *atheistic religiosity*[5] and the people's deepest beliefs, or people's truth claims, is the reproduction of the same modern liberal tradition of peaceful coexistence that antidevelopmentists so readily criticize. According to the liberal tradition, social cohesion in modern, multicultural and democratic society is not a function of *substantial* agreement between the individual members of a society but a tacit and procedural agreement that would allow each person to pursue his beliefs within the limits of his or her own private life. The only difference between these two apparently divergent perspectives is that in the case of the antidevelopment discourse the sphere of the "private" is reclaimed for each individual community, in the context of its relation with other communities – and not for each individual member.

Differently than what antidevelopmentists argue, the first step towards the transformation of the unequal relations that development has promoted is the recognition that what is at stake in the direct and indirect interventions carried

---

4   In this regard, see, for instance, Fenelon and Hall (2008) for a discussion of some of the truth claims and values that have defined the indigenous identity and self-perception.

5   I am borrowing the term from Bloom (1988).

out by development is not a clash of values nor a clash of power but a clash of truth claims. And claims to the truth cannot be tamed, restrained or silenced. They have to be contested, questioned, reasoned with, and eventually proven wrong or redeemed. It is only a disagreement over a redeemable claim that has the potential of coming to terms, even if for a period of time this would have to be a minimal agreement on listening to each other's questionable claims.

Opposing values, on the other hand, cannot come to terms. They can only be asserted against each other. Consequently, the society that displays more strength and is more willing to use it, as history has showed us, is the one that will succeed in spreading its values. If human diversity is merely a contingent reality, and not the expression of a transcendent condition that can in principle be sought after, understood and validated, what normative ground is left for one to denounce cultural invasions and development interventions?

Luckily for the cause of free and equal coexistence, human condition is such that communication and mutual understanding are built on claims that have the pretension of universal validity and *should*, therefore, have their validity continuously questioned. Agreements on the truth can certainly be manipulated and fabricated to benefit one or another established power. It is necessary, for this reason, to continuously look and ask for the conditions of possibility of mutual agreement, so that power is forced into an all-inclusive legitimization process. Before I look at the relationship between truth claims and power, which will be done in the second part of this book, let me review the third claim of the development debate and reflect on the conditions of possibility of this and the previous ones – a reflection which will then set the stage for the re-definition of social development that I carry in the third and final part of this book.

On Poverty and Recognition

Among the many controversial claims raised by both sides in the debate, there is one that stands out not only because of its novelty but especially because without it development could not be. "Global poverty", as it has been named, is a relatively new invention or "discovery".[6] For development planners and financing agencies global poverty is an undeniable fact.[7] It can be explained in relative or absolute terms but it is not a democratic or consensual condition, its existence does not depend on how the "poor" define themselves. Poverty is not a social or value construction, a reality that depends on the preferences of those affected by it. It is as real and acute as a chronic disease and it has to be eliminated.

---

6   Authors like, Sahlins (1986); Sachs (1992), Sachs (1993) and Escobar (1995) have made a rich analysis of how global poverty have come to be, not as a factual reality but as a social construct.

7   The relatively more recent work of Sachs (2005) is a well-rounded representation of this way of thinking.

Development actions are always justified in terms of overcoming poverty, to the point that many times these ideas become one.[8] The range of human goods and activities that poverty address are diverse. It can refer to a simple lack of material goods, to a lack of health services or educational opportunities. Poverty, however, is the *sine qua non* condition of development. The latter is only claimed in the presence of the first.

In this context it is crucial to ask about the condition of poverty. Can poverty be universally validated or is it only a value construction, as those who criticize development would argue? More important than challenging the legitimacy of development policies, questioning the normative status of poverty can set the idea of "development" free from the limiting chains of poverty. Development may thus result in a wealth of historically and socially unthought-of possibilities.

It is fairly easy to understand that poverty is a value construction. Even pro development literature, while treating poverty as an objective reality, is not able to conceal its fundamentally contingent nature. Although in more recent literature it becomes harder to visualize it, the poor has for a long time been identified as the individual or the society that does not have those things or those skills valued by others, that is, which other people are willing to buy at high rates.[9] Poverty thus is a condition that depends on the judgment and norms of a particular group of others.

For this simple reason development's project unilateral conceptualization of poverty, as if it belongs to the realm of the objective, observable and measurable reality, is a practical and conceptual mistake. It chooses to ignore the diversity of norms and values in human life and that anyone, therefore, can be endowed with attributes and possessions that may or may not be valued by somebody else. Poverty does not lend itself to unilateral substantial definitions – unless of course its condition of possibility is overlooked, as in fact it is.

The concept of poverty in the development project, having been established unilaterally, refers less to the conditions of the "poor" places of the world than to the reality, values, norms and beliefs of those places that have named others as poor. The invention of the Third World, though it has affected people's self-image everywhere, tell us more about the Western, industrialized and white people than about the African, Latin Americans or Asians. This is why, as critics of development point out, it is important to ask who is defining whom as poor and with what qualifications.[10] In fact, it would not require much work to identify attributes, skills and patterns of behavior that "developing" countries value and which cannot be found in the "developed" world.

The most immediate practical implication of such awareness to established patterns of international relations would be the recognition of the right of the

---

8 The work of Sachs (2005) serves again as a good example of a non-problematic, symbiotic usage of these terms.

9 Pendell (1951).

10 See, for instance, Rahnema (1992), Illich (1992) and Sachs (1993).

so-called "Third World" or "developing" countries to name and identify the values and attributes that the "First World" lacks and the legitimization of the "Third World's" actual intervention in the former "developed" countries to aid and alleviate their poverty.

Having said so, however, the influence of development could not be challenged by the simple reduction of the status of poverty to a value construction. As I have mentioned earlier, the equation of power with power alone cannot control or place any demands on power. Only if poverty entails a claim that could also be universally validated, can the legitimacy of development's factual power be questioned.

I want to argue here that poverty has been empowering development theory and practice all over the world because it addresses, among other things, a non-contingent condition of human existence. It is well-established that the value of reality for human beings is a function of their cultural processes. In other words, the value of our actions and the external reality around us comes from what each people in association with others have learned to attribute meaning to. Thus what is valuable in a community may not be in another one or at a different time. This socially and culturally determined reality entails, however, a universal human condition.

As some Critical theorists have explained it, value and meaning are the function of relations of recognition between kindred.[11] Hence poverty is an ever-present possibility because people look for mutual recognition. Outside this context, comparisons and valuations would be purposeless. Furthermore, since the equal redistribution of the products of human labor and the symbols of recognition is not a practical possibility, poverty is an ever present reality. "Global poverty" is how modern development happens to call the uneven distribution of particular material and non-material symbols within and between communities of recognition.

Critics of development question the legitimacy of the development power by challenging developmentists' claim to the truth of poverty. This questioning, although correct in identifying the content of poverty as a social construct, overlooks the condition of possibility of poverty itself. Antidevelopmentists' critique reduces the legitimacy of power to the contingency of a superior power. Because antidevelopmentists overlook the universal structure of poverty, they only go as far as to question the invention of *global* poverty, leaving the original power of development untouched.

The authority that the white Western man has attributed to himself to determine what poverty is and who the poor are is the tip of the oppression iceberg. Before he could do so, and for him to do it, he first had to establish a certain pattern according to which he could recognize the peoples of the world and be, in turn, recognized by them. It is this authority to determine the terms of an on-going

---

11   For an in-depth analysis of the structure of human relations in terms of the mutual need for recognition see Honneth (1995).

and global relation of recognition that would have to be questioned before other manifestations of power can be delegitimized.

We are all too well familiar with the historically unchallenged argument that "might make right" and its far from ideal consequences. If the idea of global poverty, however, is to be fundamentally and rationally challenged, it is not enough to denounce it as a Western invention. We also have to identify the normative conditions that have empowered global poverty in the first place and establish reasonable criteria to evaluate and re-direct its practical purpose and applications.

Oppression goes beyond and starts before the naming of the poor *outside* one's sphere of (questionable) authority. To denounce the oppression of external interference alone, while authorizing internal powers to define what is socially valuable and the criteria for the redistribution of these material and non-material goods, as antidevelopmentists do, does not tap into the roots of oppression. Overcoming the oppressive power of development requires more than evidencing the uses and misuses of a project that only looses legitimacy when trespassing its rightful limits. These are the limits of the community that *already* subscribes to particular values: those privileged by the established local power.

While the structure or the condition of possibility of poverty remains silenced by the power of development and ignored by the self-contradictory discourse of antidevelopmentists, it is unlikely that the promise of development will lose sway over the peoples of the world. The *sine qua non* condition for any social change that meets the reciprocity principle is searching for those conditions and claims that can be universalized but that the established power, either global or local, have had to fragment in order to maintain itself.

Chapter 2
The Condition Beneath the Claims:
Understanding Human Unity

I have argued in the previous section that although poverty is explained by developmentists in terms of an independent truth and, on the other hand, as a value construction by antidevelopmentists, it should, nevertheless, be understood as a value construction that is made possible due to a universal condition proper to human beings. One way of defining this condition is in terms of the human need for mutual recognition. In this chapter I want to explain the structure of this normative condition and why awareness of it can affect the modern project of development and signal a way out of the current circular and non-prolific debate that has been established over it.

Relations of recognition are purpose oriented, that is, non-arbitrary actions. They allow each person to establish a self-relation and to gradually understand, define and exercise the attributes of the self. At the collective level, these relations shape collective identities and maintain social cohesion. Through the recognition that we give and receive from each other, both our individualities and cultures are formed. Without peer recognition, there would be no self-relation and self-awareness.

Whether we understand ourselves and simultaneously perceive the other in more positive or negative terms, attributing to the self and to the other laudable attributes or not, we cannot know who we are, what we need, what we value alone, outside a community of recognition. This condition does not depend on personal choices, preferences or cultural values. It is a reality that, no matter how much we try to avoid, will always bind us and bring us back together.[1]

Human beings in every society and at any time need each other's recognition to develop their self-relation. What do change are people's reasonable expectations for being recognized in one way or another and the possibilities of recognition that are socially available. At any given time, the material and ideological

---

1 See Honneth (1995) and Taylor (1995 and 2000) for a detailed analysis of how the universal need for recognition is shaped through the historical developments of each time, and particularly in the modern time. These developments are, in their turn, the result of peoples' ongoing struggles for recognition.

circumstances of society define the prevailing patterns of recognition or the criteria for identifying the legitimacy of diverse and many times conflicting social claims and expectations.

In the modern history of European and Western societies, a pattern of recognition has developed that has legitimized people's claim for the recognition of their individual or communal, mainly national, *singularity* or their *unique* identity. This modern claim has thrived through what some have described as a tri-partied model of social recognition that has gradually and simultaneously been validated at the interpersonal, legal and economic spheres of modern life.[2]

It is more or less agreed that in Modern times and in Western and non-Western societies alike, the fulfillment of personal and/or collective unique identities is an important aspect of people's expectations. This expectation highlights the value of social recognition and empowers modern social movements with a new language. But in spite of the visibility that particular struggles for recognition have gained in Modern times, it is recognition in its most basic structure and universality that I find most relevant for the purposes of moving the debate over development forward.

Although disrespecting the need for recognition of the African people in America 500 years ago would not have the same legal, social and personal consequences as disrespecting it nowadays, denouncing different forms of social disrespect to people's growing and legitimate demand for recognition is not enough to question the foundations of the present social order. If the *structure* of power relations is to change, this questioning must also be carried out in increased approximation to the *universal,* though only historically made evident, requirements of recognition.

The Need for Recognition and Self-understanding

Since the patterns of recognition or people's social expectations are culturally bound, the discussion of an "ideal" form of recognition is at best a daunting task. I do not overlook this fact. However, in line with the work of other procedural philosophers, I want to suggest that the "ideal" can be discussed at the structural level alone,[3] in this case as a search for the *normative structure* of recognition.

Political philosophers have to be particularly alert to the potential dangers of their efforts to determine a normative framework for the study of social affairs. The systematization of a theory of recognition with the purpose of explaining people's expectations within modern capitalist societies is no exception to this rule.[4] Theories of recognition, like other critical theories, have been mainly elaborated from the perspective of the "developed" white Western man, and are for this reason an easy target for trying to disguise contingent power under universal truth.

---

2   See Honneth's theory of recognition (1995, 2003).
3   See, for instance, Honneth and Joas (1988) and Habermas (1990b).
4   See Honneth (1995) and Hartmann and Honneth (2006).

To answer these honest suspicions it is important not to lose sight of the diversity and the historical limitations of existing patterns of recognition. But if the *structure* of the prevailing power relation or established patterns of recognition is to be delegitimized and an alternative structure validated, historical awareness and analysis has to simultaneously reveal an increasingly approximated picture of the *ideal* structure of recognition. This approximation to a still not institutionalized ideal which paradoxically reveals itself through the contingency of history is the only means for questioning the legitimacy of dominant power relations.

Regardless of the particular time and society in which people live, the ideal expression of the need for recognition is an expanding self-understanding. Although I am speaking here of self-understanding in a non-specific way, this expansion is expressed in growing social inclusion and recognition. Thanks to the historically recent discourse of Modernity we can also explain self-understanding as a search that is to certain extent unique for each self, either individual or collective. The modernization of societies, for instance, claims to have favored an *in facto* diversification of the individual self or increased individuation.[5]

Although Modernity and globalization makes this human condition evident, the struggle to know and assert the unique attributes of the self have been an on-going characteristic of people at all times and in all societies.[6] People have associated with one another not simply to survive or even to be recognized and accepted, but mainly to be recognized in a certain way, that is, to know their self in a certain ideal way and thus to be able to respond for their actions in the on-going relations that they partake. Relationships of recognition determine the content, the purpose and the social value of peoples' material and cultural productions, therefore the particular way in which each people justify and understand their collective and/or individual existence. In its turn, each current stage of people's self-understanding actively and continuously shapes, redefines and transforms the established patterns of social recognition.

The factual ongoing presence of *struggles* for recognition in every society speaks of people's dissatisfaction with how recognition is at each moment fulfilling its end – although it must be remembered that the absence of such struggles does not imply popular satisfaction either. These struggles and popular mobilization show, among other things, that even though people need to be recognized, the simple acknowledgement of one's existence by other individuals and one's community is not enough. One also expects to be acknowledged in a way that tells him or her something meaningful about who he or she is. And many times the acknowledgement one receives from others is far removed from one's expectations or hopes for the self – especially in an age of individual freedom,

---

5   See Honneth (1992) and Fraser and Honneth (2003).

6   I am not claiming here a substantial philosophy of history, which would require, beyond a metaphysical reflection, an extensive comparative anthropological analysis. For the purpose of my argument in this book it suffices to shape this moral intuition into a rational (redeemable) argument.

where the dividing line between what constitutes a legitimate expectation and an illegitimate one is at best flexible and negotiable.

On the other hand, our active involvement in the struggle, our refusal to simply quit either the struggle or social coexistence all together, show us that self-definition alone, independently from the other's recognition, will not do. It is so not only because the other's recognition has something to say about our self but because we cannot even conceive this self, its powers, limitations, wants and dislikes without the other.[7] Hence, though any kind of recognition is not acceptable, recognition is the only way to assert and shape our selves. There is no direct access to oneself but the other is needed in the recognition that he/she has to offer to the awareness of personal and collective capacities – and not for the recognition that his or her simple presence offers.

The need for recognition and the need to know who we are define together another human condition: our *unity*. In broad terms, unity can be defined as a condition of equality and interdependence. To say that human beings are united means that they are *equal* in their search for self-understanding and that they *equally depend* on each other's recognition for the fulfillment of this search. Thus conceptualized, human unity has a practical political consequence: the equality that characterizes human beings, or human communities, starts as a *potential* which can only be fulfilled to the extent that *all* the parts that share this equality, that is, all human beings, are fulfilling it.

Unity at any level, human or not, is an entity or a whole, composed of individual parts – each with its particular characteristics – and defined by an integrated set of characteristics that result from the interaction between the individual characteristics of each of its members. Different levels of unity, and the corresponding status of membership, can be determined by identifying the mutual affect that different individual units have on each other. To the degree that individual units affect each other, that is, cooperate intentionally or not, *and* create an entity with new attributes, functions or capacities that are different from the simple sum of each entity's attributes, we say that these individual entities are united. In other words, at a certain level of their existence, these individual and apparently self-referential units are interdependent on each other for the fulfillment of this equality of condition, that is, their equal belonging to the larger whole.

Unity is well expressed in the metaphor of the human body. The body can be defined as a unity because its characteristics or functions depend on the way other entities come together and mutually inflect each other's individual performance. The body is capable of growing, reproducing, moving, holding objects, hearing, seeing and so on because each and all of the individual members of the body, hands, legs, eyes, internal organs, etc, contribute to *all* the functions of the body. In other words, each affects *all* the other members in their particular contributions to the functioning of the body. This does not mean that one organ cannot function without the other. In the absence of one or some members, other members may

---

7   See Taylor (2000, 2004).

still be able to perform and many times outperform their original capacities. The leg will still be able to walk and express its particularities even when the eye cannot see or the hand cannot hold. The ailment of a member, nonetheless, will of necessity affect the leg in those conditions and capacities that define its membership to the whole. In this case the leg could no longer be defined in terms of those capabilities that only had value and meaning in the context of a body able to perform a set of integrated actions. As the action of the body is limited with the ailment of one of its members, so is the meaning and the value of the leg's actions. Any organ of the body that ceases to contribute to the whole, affects all the other members in their capacity to contribute to the functioning of the body, affecting thus the purpose of each member's actions. The best performance of each member depends on the contribution of all members to each and every member's efforts to keep the healthy functioning of the body.

The metaphor of the human body evidently gives raise to intricate questions about the unity of humanity. Questions such as what are the ideal characteristics and capabilities of the entity we define as *humanity*; what are the criteria for determining membership to this humanity and how can the ideal contribution of every member to the whole of humanity be determined? And, finally, what are the implications of this reflection on human unity for the critique and transformation of the development project?

To reflect on these questions, it is important, first of all, to direct our attention to the argument that unity is a condition that may happen simultaneously at distinct superseding and overlapping levels for each entity. In the case of human beings, they simultaneously share, for instance, their physical condition with every other living creature and a cultural/social condition with the particular members of their community. The first determines the unity of all living beings, while the second may determine the unity of a nation, a people, a social group or a family. Each community has traits and characteristics that provide for a common condition or equality among its members and sets them apart from the members of another community. These characteristics and attributes of the whole, moreover, are, in ideal terms, the result of each and every member's particular contributions to the whole.

When discussing the condition of *human* unity, we are thinking of an overarching level of unity that involves all human beings, regardless of the other particular associations to which they belong. To say that all human beings are united *qua* human means that the humanity of each person depends on everybody else being granted the opportunity to contribute to the fulfillment of everyone else's humanity. This level of unity is by definition all-encompassing. The quality of this association affects and determines the possibilities of every other association we participate in. All other levels of unity, national, cultural, religious, familial, economic, etc., are made possible thanks to this most basic unity of people as human beings[8] – regardless of whether this unity manifests itself in global or local relations.

In the context of my earlier definition of human unity, we can say that the diversity of human cultures and life styles are the result of people's interdependence in their search for understanding through mutual recognition. Although the characteristics that in principle everyone shares in their common condition as humans are not and cannot be substantially defined, there is still room to talk about the general characteristics of these commonalities. If it were not for the most basic condition of interdependency in the search for self-understanding, there would be no culture, values or relative truths. Every human creation exists and gains value and meaning within a community of kindred that shares these two basic conditions. These conditions unite the members of a community not only as Muslims, African-Americans or Brazilians but also as human beings.

This definition of human unity implies that people's universally shared humanity becomes the condition of possibility of diversity. No cultural manifestation could exist if it was not for the existence of beings with a common condition that, in need of each other, would come together to bring to fruition this condition. In the struggle to fulfill their search for self-understanding, human beings shape a diversity of meaningful and valuable realities within their interactions. Other levels of unity, such as cultural, national or religious, with their specific values and patterns of recognition, are possible thanks to this all-encompassing unity at the human level. In other words, human beings, regardless of their particular affiliations and identities and the time and space that they inhabit, universally share those basic conditions necessary for the creation of culture and for being simultaneously shaped by it.

The Limits of the Community of Recognition

The discussion of human unity renews the question of membership that political thinkers have for long now pursued and seek to answer: to whom should the right be given to associate in the constitution of a particular society and whom, on this basis, could be legitimately excluded? Even if we accept the existence of a universal humanity beyond and above particular humanities, the issue of whose recognition is relevant for the shaping of one's particular humanity and who should thus be included in the community that in actuality shapes people's personality may still be left unanswered.[9]

---

8   In the context of this argument see Bevir (2001) for an interesting discussion on how, for Derrida, unconditional friendship is the condition of possibility for local and conditional relations of friendship. I will discuss this topic in more detail in the third part.

9   See Nussbaum and Cohen (1996) and Nussbaum (1997) for an example of a historically bound justification of world citizenship. From her perspective human unity is a modern phenomenon, brought about by globalization. Membership to the global

Putting the question of membership into the context of the development debate, antidevelopmentists would say at this point in my argument that the idea of "humanity" overlooks the diversity of cultures and the need thereof for particular forms of recognition, which cannot, moreover, be reconciled. The argument that people share the capacity to produce cultures does not imply that people *should* work and cooperate together, as members of a universal society. People only need the positive recognition of the members of their own community. Concomitantly, they should try to avoid the negative impact that other cultures' patterns of recognition may have on them. Because cultures usually do not share the same set of values and social symbols, the recognition they have to offer to each other would be far-off from the particular ways each would like to assert itself and hopes, therefore, to be recognized.

The idea that human beings are united as members of a single humanity is not an invitation to cooperation and integration. If anything it serves more as a warning for societies to keep their distance from each other's cultural and political borders. The idea of a common humanity, even if accepted, could enforce antidevelopmentists' practical demand that the self-understanding of each people, and their respective descriptions of reality, be defined by each community alone.[10] This would hold true especially for those societies whose values and traditions, or self-image and capacities, have been systematically threatened and impaired by the recognition of an "other" who has taken the universality of its own patterns of recognition for granted.

In response to these objections, it is important to remember that although people have historically recognized each other in negative terms, this is not the *only* recognition that they can give and receive. Negative and downgrading forms of recognition, though a historical truth, are not a self-explanatory reality. The fact that people can and have affected each other negatively reflects a broader condition: their condition of unity or interdependency. It is because of our unity in our condition as humans that we can affect each other's humanity in such destructive ways, even when we so significantly differ from each other in every aspect of our existence.

In setting criteria for determining the oppressive nature of human action in general and those carried more recently by development theory and practice, in

---

community, therefore, is explained purely in contingent terms: people happen to affect each other's life in this time and age and, therefore, their decisions should take others into account. But humanity, as a child of globalization, is a post facto event that places a moral claim on the peoples of the world based on the irreversibility of globalization's power. This power based justification of what people ought to do is indeed, as antidevelopmentists and post-modernists would correctly denounce oppression under the guise of humanism. But differently from antidevelopmentists, I argue that we should do more than reveal the claim to power hidden beneath moral claims. We should also ask what is hidden beneath the claim to power.

10   See, for instance, Esteva (2009).

particular, it is crucial that we look for that condition that made these actions possible. Revealing this condition help us understand how oppression was possible in the first place and how, concomitantly, oppression could have been and can be avoided.

The more we recognize and respect the condition of unity, the more we are able to express the diversity of our individual and collective selves. Our unity tells us of possibilities that would not be known to us otherwise. It tells us about the meaning and the value of our diverse actions and choices when we decide to put them at the service of other people and be served by them. Our unity can tell us much more than we would ever know, were we to remain closed to the ways that the diversity of others interacts with ours. It is to the extent that we are able to see our particular cultures in the context of our human unity that we can give expression to its full potentiality, a potentiality that remains dormant until the other can show us how real, needed and valuable our culture is.

It is in this context that we need to understand oppression, which has been more recently identified and denounced in the process of globalization, a process greatly supported by the theory and practice of development. Globalization, contrary to what antidevelopmentists argue, is not oppressive in absolute terms. So far it has evidently promoted relationships that have denied the value of cultural diversity and defeated even the meekest awareness of people's wealth. It has showed many that what they knew and how they behaved was purposeless and socially irrelevant.[11] Correspondingly, it has asserted to a few that the value of their knowledge, production and behavior was self-referential, that their values stood on their own and that they could and should not be valued nor validated, and consequently altered, within all-inclusive relations of interdependency and mutual recognition.

Globalization has, in short, significantly limited the self-understanding and destroyed or reduced the practical capabilities of everyone and every community in the world, the so called developed and underdeveloped alike. This is not, however, all that globalization can afford.

The Globalization Process

From the perspective of human unity, the globalization process represents a change in those material conditions of the world that allows for an increased recognition of our fundamental unity. Globalization, whether in its economic or cultural expressions, has established global relations that have increased the possibility of understanding human unity and of *intentionally* respecting (or disrespecting) it.

---

11   See Quijano (2000), Maalouf (2000), Makhijani (2003) and Berman (2006) for a discussion of how different peoples have been similarly affected in their self-perception by the patterns of recognition that have been established originally by and in relation with the European man and later on with the so called developed world.

As it happens with any universal condition that becomes gradually manifest, the challenges and opportunities that come along with such acknowledgement also increase. It is not that globalization suddenly unites us all or that unity becomes truer now than it has been before, as some political philosophers have argued.[12] The risks and opportunities that come along with globalization are of a different nature. Human beings have always shared the condition of humanity, that which makes them exclusively human, and this truth has been argued in different ways for thousands of years.[13] What occurs in modern times, initially with the European colonization and then with what we nowadays call the globalization of the economy and elements of the Western culture, is that it brings all human beings, not only a few enlightened ones, to the threshold of this understanding. Globalization, therefore, gives everyone for the first time in history the opportunity to harvest the fruits of human unity.

Globalization shows people everywhere the possibilities of unity, how it can affect and how it is affecting their lives. If before these changes people were simply living under this condition, unity no longer unceasingly pour its favors, or at least some of its benefits, upon us. Fully revealed in its inclusiveness and no longer dormant and inoffensive, it becomes continuously threatened with disrespect, threatening our self-relation in return. While the material circumstances and patterns of thought that have gradually evolved allow for an increased awareness of our unity, releasing thus unprecedented human capacities, these circumstances also increase the possibilities of disrespect to human unity and the threats to people's self-relation that results thereof.

The indigenous people in America were evidently safer in their self-relation before receiving the recognition of fellow Europeans – and being submitted to the relations of power that were derived from this recognition. Their lives, traditions, values, and eventually their life style became gradually threatened as they entered or were forced into relationships defined by new patterns of recognition. This experience may not have told them directly of the unity of humanity but it made such understanding possible as some of its consequences became clear. The encounter tells the indigenous people about a white man that, although they had not met before and whose existence was of no apparent consequence to them, is now crucially affecting their self-understanding. An invasion of locusts that had destroyed their source of material existence and put their life at risk could not have affected their community in the same profound and irreversible manner. It would have told them about the level of animal unity in which they participate, a unity that keeps all living beings connected and where the action of one affects the physical survival of all others. But the white man's invasion affected their self-understanding as members of a different kind of relation, a relation that affects precisely one's capacity to define the self. While the first invasion allows for an

---

12   See, for instance, Nussbaum (1997), Appiah (2006) and Benhabib (2006).

13   For an analysis of the history of world citizenship and the idea of a common humanity in the Western thought see the detailed work of Heater (1996).

understanding of the attributes of the self that are shared with other living creatures, the second questions the very condition of possibility of this and every other understanding. As a matter of fact, one of the understandings that the colonizers' pattern of recognition challenges is the indigenous people's understanding that the self shares a common condition with all other living creatures. Eventually self-understanding as a whole is affected. And so, though less frequently discussed, is the white man's self-understanding.

Although increased globalization is not enough to materialize the reality of human unity into a politics of universal symmetrical inclusion where everyone's self-understanding is positively affected and expanded, the encounter between different cultures is the *sine qua non* condition for such materialization and, concomitantly, for an expanded self-relation, both at the individual and group level. To understand why and how this happens, it is important to explain the function of *social symbols* in the process of self-understanding.

The self, whether individual or collective, is differentiated and gains awareness within communities of recognition characterized by pre-validated patterns of thought, norms, and behaviors. These material and non-material production, proper to all human societies, can be called social symbols or symbols of recognition. Social symbols differentiate one community from another and determine how each individual member will be recognized within his or her own community and develop a self-relation.

Social symbols represent the achievements of a particular community and work as the foundation for the development of new ones. The production and distribution of these symbols are the materialization of the process of self-knowledge or self-realization. This positive role of social symbols is threatened, however, by the tendency that all societies manifest to gradually consolidate their symbols into the status of an unquestionable truth. When this happens social symbols cease to be the expression of the interplay of the totality of capacities that constitutes a particular society, in a particular moment, and instead begin to limit the understanding and reduce the expression of people's capacities. When social symbols gain a status independent from the condition that makes them possible – the human need for recognition in his or her search for self-understanding – they start to curtail rather than to expand the capacities of those who produce them and express their selves through this production.

The encounter with the other, and not only recent encounters but any cultural shock that has happened throughout the history of human societies, enables the revision of our self-image and understanding, as it forces us into questioning the status of our social symbols. Going back to the example of the human body, each encounter reveals to parts of the body that their capacities are not complete, that they can be integrated and enhanced, serve and be served by the other's – until then unmet – capacities. The leg would find out in each cultural shock, so to speak, that it has an eye, hands, toes, etc. It would find out that the things it had done and the way it had done them are not the only or the best way that things can be done. It would discover, moreover, that many of the things that it had previously done have a greater value and meaning than it could, in isolation and by itself, have ever imagined.

Every cultural shock, at the collective or individual levels, asks the involved parties to question the validity of their own symbols and to possibly validate new ones. To the extent that the parties succeed in doing so they turn the mere reproduction of symbols into an individual and collective realization of increasingly unique and diversified capacities. Self-awareness expands with the realization that routine and well-established norms, patterns of thought and behavior do and should fulfill purposes other than guaranteeing the preservation of social order and the granting of social recognition to individual members.

In the sense that it offers the concrete possibility for questioning every social symbol all over the world, globalization is a positive development. The cultural shock that it entails rightly raises questions about the limits of the community of recognition in an age when all are subject to the evaluative gaze of everyone else. Social symbols are confronted, their traditional truths threatened and people empowered with the initial but unassailable requirement for overcoming the oppression of self-referential local and global symbols.

It is important to stress that I am not defending economic and cultural globalization as a process that fosters respect to human unity. The economic interdependency that globalization promotes can and should be questioned. It is not a universal condition as its defenders, those who benefit from the power of globalization, claim. It is certainly a powerful event, shaping and re-defining the collective and individual self of billions of people around the world. But it is not an exercise of power that can coherently legitimize itself as fostering respect to a universal condition.

As we will see in detail in the next chapter, current trends of globalization only address part of our human condition, while trying to convince people – if necessary with threats of marginalization, exclusion and withdrawal of recognition – that they stand for a self-explanatory and self-sufficient reality. The globalization process speaks to our need for recognition but imposes it as an end in itself. Social acceptance detached from a legitimate search for self-understanding, leads to dichotomized relations, those of dependency, instead of interdependence and between superiors and inferiors instead of equals.

Although our need for recognition is real and, therefore, very appealing to us whenever and wherever it is evoked, this is a mutual need and never one sided. Because it is driven towards the expansion of self-understanding, it can only be expressed within a symmetrical relation. When development discourse and practice tries to promote economic growth equating it with human development, it is addressing our need for recognition *as if* it is a self-referential and asymmetrical relation, *as if* it could be fulfilled by simply giving to people the possibility of accumulating the symbols that development has deemed worth valuing. Such discourse may well have gone unchallenged, had it belonged to a different age, one that had not gone through the pains of universalizing the right of *all* to search for self-understanding.

Globalization, which builds its rationale mainly on elements of the development discourse and is materialized through so called development strategies, has showed to people a certain different image of their selves. In this sense, and only in this one, globalization is a done deal, a process without return. Once we see ourselves in a new way, through the gaze of the other, we cannot simply pretend that we have not seen – in an act of psychotic delusion – what we know we have just seen. Even if for a flickering moment, the glance of the unknown and his gaze will forever stay with us and change us without return, as colonizers or colonized, oppressors or oppressed. The fact that we may accept, inquire or altogether reject the new image, does not change the effect that it causes on us, the seed of doubt that it instills, questioning the value of an until then omniscient self.

This is why the question that antidevelopmentists pose as to whose recognition communities need or would benefit from has no practical consequences nor carries any empowering promise. We have no longer the choice to decide whether the Western white man's recognition is something that we desire or not. His recognition has affected everyone, starting some five hundred years ago with the great encounter.

The global reach of the Western man's gaze goes beyond the gradual globalization of the Western, white, male, modern and Christian symbols of recognition and even beyond his material power to impose these symbols on everybody else. This trend, that is, globalization, cannot, by itself, curtail a return to the isolation and self-sustaining life of communities before the Modern era, as some antidevelopmentists correctly point out but mistakenly hope for.[14]

The terms and characteristics of the economic, political and cultural globalization of the world should and will surely be redefined as people are empowered with a new sense of their interdependency and worth. But to wish for a relationship of recognition that excludes all or parts of what different cultures have to say to each other, in the name of how oppressive this recognition has been, is to ignore the impact of human unity in the age of globalization. At the very moment of the encounter or the cultural shock between symbols that, not knowing about each other, had reigned supreme and absolute, our historical humanity, or our universal capacity to collectively create and attribute meaning and value to reality, reveals itself, de-stabilizing our self-image and changing us forever.

The awareness, made possible by globalization, that human beings are united at the level of their self-understanding is empowering to people everywhere because it redefines the bonds of recognition in terms of fundamental equality. Unlike the patterns of recognition that globalization currently tries to legitimize and impose, the need for recognition that itself helps to reveal, binds people in a relation of universal reciprocity, that is, in a relation which normative structure is of absolute symmetry.

Globalization and the development project deny this fundamental reciprocity and universality while the antidevelopment discourse indirectly accepts and

---

14   See, for instance, Illich (1980), Sachs (1997) and Esteva and Prakash (1998).

complies with this denial. Globalization, thus approached, seems to have won after all. The distorted picture of reality that it presents, one ruled only by the asymmetrical need for recognition, remains unchallenged. Critics are unwilling to go beyond its core assumptions. No resistance is shown against the truth claims made by its power, no demands made for a power that must coherently convince *everyone* of its legitimacy. The struggle between those who favor and those who are against globalization seems to be reduced to the battlefield of power, to the best strategy for confining power within the limits of pre-established authority. Since this strategy does not question the validity of the claims that power raises to legitimize or authorize itself, the debate between the two sides does nothing but to perpetuate the same patterns of legitimacy and thus the same structure of power already in place.

A reflection into the normative structure of recognition can show us that it implies equal dependency between participants; that it is not self-serving – it is a relation that has to constantly re-adjust itself, revealing a search that goes beyond fulfilling the need for recognition alone; and that it is all-inclusive. As a means for achieving self-understanding, recognition cannot create relations of dependency nor independence. At the moment a person associates with another he or she is engaging in a search for recognition which purpose, self-understanding, can only be achieved as long as no one is in principle excluded from it and as long as all the involved are equally expanding their self-understanding.

Recognition evidently serves diverse contingent and finite purposes, as revealed by the fact that people participate in many different associations during their lifetime. We may also reasonably expect that as the common purposes that bring people together and create equal dependence between nations, consumers and producers, husband and wife and so on so forth, cease to exist, so will these free associations. Nonetheless, because *all* human relations can be subsumed, directly or indirectly, under the overarching purpose of self-understanding, in a way relations of recognition also bind people inescapably – and thus universally – together.

A person may, for instance, cease to need the recognition of another as a market player but he or she will never overcome the need for recognition that the other has to offer as a human, to his or her humanity. It is the possibility of this unconditional recognition that gives meaning to the choice of playing the role of a financial actor in the first place. The human bond that unites people or their equal need for unconditional recognition in order to fulfill their particular search for self-understanding, will continuously ask for the other in his or her universality, and not in his or her particularities. The unity of the people at the level of their humanity, a fundamental relation that gives meaning and explain all other forms of association or from which all other levels of unity derive, determines a universal relation of recognition that persists despite the rise and fall of all other forms of association.

So far I have explained the meaning of unity and how this fundamental and non-contingent reality, although benefiting from processes of modern globalization, justifies inclusiveness in terms other than globalization does. In the reality of daily life, nonetheless, social interactions, more often than not, happen in an asymmetrical way, conferring to iniquity and dependency – and not to human interdependency – the status of reality. The condition of human unity, which is the requirement of any relation, including those of oppression, is seldom questioned, sought after and made evident.

In the next chapter I will explore the implications of the condition of unity for the re-definition of human relations in general and for the relation between developed and developing countries in particular. This analysis is done in two parts: 1) recognition is defined in terms of two normative categories, moral and ethical – this differentiation sets the ground for determining how relations of dependency affect people in developing and developed countries in regards to their self-understanding; and 2) the core claims raised in the development debate – freedom, values and poverty – are re-conceptualized from the perspective of people's fundamental unity.

Chapter 3
Beyond Dependency: A Recognition Approach to the Development Debate

The need for mutual recognition and self-understanding – which defines the unity of human beings – determines that beyond every human relation, equal or unequal, there is an unconditional one that will always be the condition of possibility of all other relations. It is at this unconditional, fundamental and, simultaneously, ideal level of interaction that human beings are and will remain equal. At this level of interaction, every action has a symmetrical effect on all human beings, regardless of practical exclusions and practical asymmetries.

Every human relation embodies concurrently different spheres of recognition. In spite of the fact that all of them *may* be expressed through unequal power relations, all are driven towards ideal equality. The absence of factual equality does not mean that one side is fulfilling his need for self-understanding more or less than the other is. It just manifests the temporary predominance of certain social symbols in the context of relationships which are not meaningful and fulfilling to either side. Self-understanding is necessarily an all-inclusive process.

Relations of Dependency

To understand how unequal relations of dependency are maintained due to an original relation of interdependence, we must begin with a reflection on the means that recognition uses to manifest itself. The process of giving and receiving recognition and expanding self-understanding does not happen in a social and historical vacuum. It is mediated by symbols, which throughout time are collectively established, consolidated and eventually transformed. These symbols are what allow for differences in the ways we recognize each other. The Portuguese and Spanish explorers that arrived at the South American shores in the sixteenth century, for instance, found a people that did not hold their symbols and did not recognize the value of these symbols as expressed in the European religious practices, language, food and clothing. The recognition of the other as a superior, an equal or an inferior that results from this encounter is necessarily mediated by the symbols that each side has learned to value and attribute meaning to.

The fact that recognition functions through the medium of social symbols is not in itself problematic, given that the original and unconditional relation of recognition that sustains a particular relation be acknowledged and respected. Under such circumstances, the conditionality of – symbol mediated – relations of recognition are evidenced as well as the practical limitations of time and space contingent social symbols in fostering self-understanding.

Social symbols are relevant to the extent that they allow the members of each community to expand their self-relation within meaningful social relations. Without these symbols, that is, practices that are commonly valued and justified, there would be no horizon of reference in relation to which the person could compare and define him or herself,[1] social relations would lose purpose and social cohesion would be threatened. It should also be noted, as we will see in a while, that social relations can only be meaningful and foster self-understanding as they become increasingly inclusive. For this reason social symbols are necessary mutable realities.

The adequacy of social symbols to their general and many particular purposes can and should be constantly questioned. Such inquiry allows each community and each person, in every new generation, to identify themselves with pre-established social symbols. Failure to question this adequacy is simultaneously a threat to personal integrity, to the unity of the community and the expansion of social solidarity. The first step in questioning how well certain symbols are fulfilling their immediate as well as their core purpose is consciousness of its contingent, "recognition dependent", condition.

Questioning social symbols is a difficult learning process for individuals and communities alike. And the source of personal and collective dependency lies precisely in this inability to question. Relations of dependency are those where the symbols around which they are established are taken for granted and satisfy, therefore, only the immediate need for recognition. They are relations based on an illusion: the illusion that the symbols have a life of their own. In this sense, the illusion belongs to all participants in the relationship. No matter how advantageous one's position is in holding certain symbols, when these are not questioned they acquire a status independent of the particular relation of recognition that gave birth to them and they do so at the cost of sacrificing the self-understanding of all participants, both of those who lack and those who hold and impose them.

From the perspective of human unity – interdependency in the attribution of meaning and value to social symbols – relations of dependency constitute one end side in the uninterrupted continuum that characterizes the process of self-understanding. Still driven towards self-understanding and ideal equality, those entangled in this type of relation pull together conclusions and interpretations that consistently distance them from the sought after end.

---

1   See Taylor (2000), for instance, for a detailed analysis of how self-relation is dependent on this horizon of reference.

From a conceptual perspective, a *relation* of dependency is a contradiction. As long as any relation exists and does not disintegrate, that is, as long as all the sides intentionally and without external threats seek each other's association, this relation is benefiting all the involved in a symmetrical way. Relations between inferiors and superiors do not have a self-sufficient existence. Some condition must be symmetrically tended to when a manifestly uneven relation is successfully maintained.

Within the condition of human unity, the answer to this riddle lies in the (co)original need for recognition. Recognition is actually being fulfilled in each and every human relation, as long as it persists – though not necessarily as the result of a exchange of recognition that happens directly between those involved in one and the same relation. When for both sides recognition is the *only* purpose looked after, the relation, regardless of its proclaimed ends, tends toward dependency. Ironically, relations of dependency are those in which both sides are trying to avoid or overcome the condition of human unity.

Although relations of recognition constitute the structure of any human relation – binding people together while shaping and defining interdependency – some relations of recognition meet their original purpose and others don't. Despite of the fact that human beings associate to fulfill different needs and desires through mutual recognition, relations of recognition have an ever faithful companion: the search for self-understanding. Every human association is driven towards an increase in self-understanding. Relationships clearly allow for different levels of understanding. In some, it is continuously expanding, diversifying human action and patterns of interaction. In others, it is very limited, restricted to the reproduction of certain symbols. The capacities of each side hardly differentiate and people's potentialities remain tied to the reproduction of the same set of social possibilities. The self remains still, enslaved to particular symbols, old or ever new ones. Its understanding of the value of social symbols for the construction of its particular biography does not expand. To the degree that the acquisition and reproduction of social symbols become the sole goal, these relations lead some to believe in their superiority and others in their inferiority, in their independence or dependency.

As human interdependency is slowly and gradually acknowledged, relations move closer to equality. A relationship that respects human unity recognizes and fulfills the capacities of all participants. Social symbols are therein perceived as the expression of people's capacities in interaction and not only as their determinant. To the extent that each self realizes its potentialities within the context of its interaction with the other's capacities, participants understand their personal capacities in the context of a more inclusive, more coherent and meaningful social existence. The relation that is aware of the origin of social symbols, is a relation that tends towards equality, not necessarily in the distribution and exchange of symbols but in the recognition of people's symmetrical dependence in the attribution of meaning and value to each other's symbols and thus in the expansion of self-understanding.

Moral and Ethical Relations of Recognition

From what has been said so far, we can now define human relations in terms of two different patterns of recognition: moral and ethical. Both patterns belong to the same continuum and as we distance ourselves from one, we get closer to the other. Moral recognition can be explained as approximations to an unconditional recognition of the other or the regulation of social interactions according to principles of universal inclusion. Ethical recognition is a conditional relation in which recognition becomes an end in itself.

Those involved in a moral relation are not free from social symbols but they are aware of its origin in relations of interdependency. They know that symbols are the product of the interaction of beings that have a diversity of capacities and who, in an effort to realize these capacities, create and re-create symbols. In moral recognition the participants are aware that symbols do not have an independent value, outside the community of recognition that attributes value and meaning to them. They are aware that it is an interaction of human potentialities that makes social symbols meaningful and not the other way around. It is not because human beings possess certain symbols or behave in a certain way that they can be recognized as equally valuable. The measure of their value is not their symbols but the capacity to create them.

Symbols raise implicit or explicit truth claims and they thrive on the assumption that these claims can be collectively validated. Though they may never be questioned, and most won't, such assumption is the background of common understanding and collective agreement. In this way shared symbols can be reproduced throughout time and social cohesion can be maintained. Symbols are not themselves, however, their own condition of possibility. They are representations of the human condition, the language that this condition uses to express itself. Through them people recognize each other and struggle to manifest their potentialities.

Concomitantly, symbols may hinder human potentialities. They may start determining the value of its holder more than vice versa, till they gradually become unquestionable, though not irreplaceable. Ironically, unquestioned symbols may be easily replaced, discarded by partial interests that are committed solely with receiving recognition. In this case processes of collective questioning and participation are deemed unnecessary because the symbol has become so detached from the context of social interactions that it turns utterly flat, devoid of all social meaning and transcendent value. Paradoxically, therefore, the more impoverished a symbol becomes the more it pre-determines the value of its holder. Without a past, their existence is taken for granted and their future is the outcome result of arbitrary struggles for recognition. As succeeding generations cease to revalidate them, they start oppressing the release of human potentialities and moral recognition is reduced to ethical recognition.

In a relation of ethical recognition social symbols gain an independent status. Recognition of the other's value is guaranteed as long as he or she holds a particular set of symbols. Here the relation between superiors and inferiors finds a palpable ground. Those who have more symbols are superior to others and assert their independence in relation to those who have less, the inferior and dependent one. The search for self-understanding is sacrificed in the altar of an easy recognition. Unable to acknowledge the condition of human unity, those participating in relations of ethical recognition struggle to achieve independence and the so-called freedom from the interference of the other. It is hoped that the acquisition of symbols will determine independence for all. This intended independence, however, only represents submission to the symbols of recognition, that is, to one's need for recognition. People's interdependency is thus unsuccessfully transferred to the dependency to social symbols.

The sought after rupture with human interdependence is an illusion. What happens, as long as social symbols are not questioned, is the reduction of one's need for recognition to an end in itself. Recognition becomes detached from its other half, the need for self-understanding, threatening the humanity in each and every one of us. A relation like this can correctly be named one of dependency – not between the one who has less towards the one who has more but the dependency of both, the superior and the inferior, to established symbols of recognition. Both sides are oppressed and made slave to this need within. Such a need, once deviated from the context and purpose that gives meaning to it, instead of releasing human capacities, reduce their expression to the blind imitation of what may be either long established or contemporary patterns of recognition.

Societies and individuals tend to solidify their interactions on ethical standards until, through a change in the material and spiritual conditions of life, learning processes move them forward towards moral relationships. Gradually moral relations harden back into ethical relations until once again these are questioned and overcome. The gradual move from ethical to moral relations does not imply stages in human history where material and non-material symbols are equally distributed. It represents a stage when the social status of these symbols – as the measure of personal and collective value – becomes readily available for public inquiry within renewed and extended relations of social inclusion. This openness and readiness to critique means that society, at a certain moment, recognizes the fundamental equality of previously excluded social groups. The latter are included as equals in the questioning that they offer to social symbols which they themselves do not share. Beyond the diversity of symbols, they are recognized as equals in their contribution to everyone's self-understanding. This expansion of recognition may eventually result in homogenized patterns of action and interaction which can again be diversified with the recognition and introduction of new social groups in one's community of recognition.

The widespread democratic attitude – a clear trait of both development and antidevelopment discourses – of simply accepting everyone's equal value without simultaneously considering the means for a collective and all-inclusive expression and validation of people's claims, is far from promoting a relationship between equals. Society engages in moral recognition when it accepts that all its members are equal in the irreplaceability of the recognition that they offer to the fulfillment of everyone else's search for self-understanding.

The acceptance of unconditional equality differs from an unquestioned acceptance of differences. People's fundamental equality implies an increasingly inclusive and diversified association in the search for the truth. When this requirement is overlooked, attachment to social symbols, emptied of any value other than guaranteeing recognition, holds the upper hand. A non-interested and non-inquisitive way of accepting the other's equality reflects society's fear of having its symbols questioned. Behind most of the development and antidevelopment discourses on democratic self-determination lies the apprehension of losing old self-images and the fear of unknown challenges that quiescent capacities give rise to.

Self-fulfillment and Self-satisfaction

The social and personal consequences of moral relations, on one hand, and ethical relations, on the other, are considerably different. While moral recognition expands social inclusion and the possibilities of recognition and differentiates self-relation, fostering self-understanding and *self-realization* for all, ethical recognition promotes social homogenization, a flattened self-relation and the *self-satisfaction* of some. Moral recognition involves interpreting social reality, expressed in the language of symbols, in a diverse and yet action coordinated manner. Ethical recognition leads to societies where the value of each and every interaction is measured more by the recognition that its symbols provide to the beholder than by their contribution to the building of a coherent life biography. The acknowledgment of human unity reflected in moral relations cultivates respect and advances the realization of people's diversity. The assertion of an absolute difference, built on irreconcilable truths, trap societies into the homogenizing reproduction of established patterns of recognition – while giving the appearance of heterogeneity by incessantly multiplying the number of meaningless social symbols.

In modern societies self-satisfaction is easily mistaken by self-realization. It is important thus to delve for a moment into their difference, especially if we are to contribute with the definition of a normative criteria for reviewing the current theory and practice of social development. The prevalence of self-satisfaction, as opposed to self-realization, can be identified indirectly through certain social symptoms. The most evident one is the growing contradiction in social symbols. As a prelude to upcoming changes, society's institutions and patterns of interaction, including discourses, norms and regulations, legitimize and work towards goals that cannot be simultaneously and coherently sustained.

Because self-satisfaction results from a pressing and overriding concern with social recognition, society and its members become ever more self-assertive and less prone to coordinate their goals and modes of action. Decision-making processes are characterized by immediacy and concreteness as social goals are captive in a space devoid of transcendence, a space where meaning looses consistency and continuity. As the symbols of each group and institution that composes society vary, so will they grow in contradiction.

A life in compliance thereof with self-satisfaction is permanently threatened with self-destruction. Each symbol must compete to assert its dominion in a sphere of symbols foreign to each other's value and aloof to each other's fate. There are no criteria for judging the value of the changes these symbols and society as a whole go through; no criteria for assessing the meaning of human choices against the wider landscape of personal and collective biographies. People are driven around by the mode of the day and approximations to one's potentialities and possibilities remain unlikely.

Self-realization is the process of knowing one's own capacities, namely, knowing their social value and realizing them in the context of an increasingly coherent life history. Such process requires the *re-appropriation* of social symbols by each member of society; that is, questioning the extent to which established social practices and patterns of behavior embody the contribution of each member and social group to the realization of the others' capacities. This attribution of personal value and meaning to collective symbols is the source of growing coherency throughout one's life.

Choices and actions cease to be determined by the need for recognition alone when the truth claims implicitly or explicitly raised by social symbols are recovered and engaged in a process of mutual validation. When this validation constitutes the basis for mutual recognition, the effort to protect one's symbols within limited communities of recognition gives way to ever more inclusive relations. Although such material expansion and diversification of *meaningful* social relations can increase the diversity of symbols, this diversity is not an indispensable result. The unequivocal result of self-realization is an increase in the understanding of the *original* meaning of one's choices and actions within expanded relations of cooperation.

The term "original" can highlight important differences in the usage and social value of "diversity". Societies may be diverse in their material and nonmaterial production and there may abound a diversity of social roles. Yet they may be homogenous and fragmented in the reasons and motivations for action that find expression therein. Diversity may hence be another tool in the struggle for recognition than a realm of possibilities for the expression of people's understanding of the original meaning of their actions and practices.

Paradoxically, it is awareness of the condition of human unity that guarantees a meaningful diversity. It is not hard to conceive that unity, by definition, requires some level of diversity. Sameness would make the constituting parts self-sufficient and thus altogether independent from each other. On the other hand, an absolute assertion of diversity – diversity without common grounds – implies the impossibility of shared criteria for questioning the validity of such diversity. The absence of such criteria, by its turn, results in the homogenization of social life, locally or at the global level. The first only differs from the second as it humbly accepts to keep social symbols within the limits of one and the same community.

Globalization is a more "arrogant" casualty of the struggle for recognition: certain symbols thrive better when imposed on everyone.

Human unity – and not imposed uniformity – means relating to the diversity of the other as an essential feature in the realization of one's own originality. When human diversity, expressed in the variety of symbols that each community produces, is acknowledged as a requirement for the understanding of the *meaning* of one's own symbols, neglecting the value of such diversity would be self-defeating. This is what happens with antidevelopmentists' claim for the isolation of the community,[2] as if other societies and their respective symbols had no fundamental contribution to make to one's own perceptions and understandings. Likewise, developmentists' claims that global projects are a necessity of the time would miss the point. The conscious realization of people's originality would require the acceptance of people's diversity within a renewed framework of association and mutual commitment.

The unity of the human condition and its diversity are constitutive of human relations and at the same time a goal to be achieved. In spite of their inalienability, unity and diversity can be disrespected, their requirements ignored and demands delegitimized. As a matter of fact, when the need for recognition becomes the prevalent reality, associations become valuable to the extent that they can satisfy private and partial interests. Human unity serves the struggle for *preserving* one's interests. Such misuse of unity is ironically justified on equalitarian basis: it is legitimate to use people as long as everybody is granted the same chance of profiting from one another. And once the interests related to a particular and contingent unity are satisfied, that association is terminated. Regardless of the interests that are sought to be fulfilled, this type of association, where people are means to fulfill mutual interests, seeks the final (and impossible) goal of freedom *from* each other. The struggle to satisfy certain interests, without regards for *understanding* these interests in relation to the other's diversity, is to accumulate enough to finally dispose of the other, or in any case, to be able to look at him as one who can at any time be excluded.

Unity cannot be altered or avoided. Disrespecting it, however, is an easy matter. It requires the consolidation of ethical patterns of recognition, that is, the reduction of our human condition to one of its basic dimensions, the need for recognition. When this need is detached from its purpose – self-realization – it can be used to justify any action and every end.

As patterns of thought and material conditions of life have brought people together, more than ever before, consequences for disrespecting human unity have become gradually and perceptibly more destructive. Before people encounter a new "other" it is not crucial for the self-understanding of the sides that their fundamental equality and interdependence be mutually recognized. And this demand has been triggered by old and modern colonization; by the globalization of the economy; by the development of modern technology and so on so forth.

---

2   See, for instance, Esteva and Prakash (1997).

An association that is consciously built on the foundation of unity is not a temporary relation between needy sides that try to extract or take from each other as much as possible to fulfill particular ends. When unity is respected, everyone's unique and irreplaceable presence is acknowledged and each side is primarily concerned with the mutual validation of individual and group's choices, that is, with mutual understanding. In this process the other is never disposable. The appreciation of his original presence constantly reveals and expands the expression of one's own capacities. The sides are aware that any loss or deprivation that any of them goes through implies everyone's loss. Unity does not allow for a win/lose relationship. Respect to this condition is a win/win situation and disrespect to it a collective lost.

It is very difficult for contemporary societies, built on ethical relations, reproducing incoherent and fragmented symbols, selling cheap self-satisfaction and promising individual salvation, to grasp and envisage the reality of human unity. However, because people *are* united there is no level of accumulation at which the other will finally not be needed anymore. As we long for an increased accumulation and display of symbols, we are over and over reminded of our ever-present need for the other.

When a symbol happens to lose its *social* value, the beholder is usually left with nothing but shambles. In this case it becomes clear that even one's selfish goals rely heavily on the social. However, even when the social value of a symbol is successfully maintained, the always present, though unacknowledged, drive to know one's own capacities, takes the beholder to engage in a continuous *social* validation of his or her symbols. When the value of a symbol is taken for granted, social validation, nonetheless, resembles the growth of a malignant tumor. The symbols that are thus "validated" grow without limits, invading other organs, unaware of the unity of the whole and eventually killing the very source of their existence. The growth of a tumor will not change the reality of unity. In actuality the tumor only grows thanks to this unity. Though unity is not in itself a barrier against total destruction, because of this unity the tumor will eventually, however, cease to exist. Its fast growth can only give the temporary illusion of an advantageous position. The unity of the body and the impossibility of a win/loose relationship, sooner or later, becomes manifest. It is evidently easy to detect the condition of unity once the growing tumor and the other organs disintegrate. The challenge, however, is to understand it before nothing else can be done. This understanding, furthermore, should not be motivated by the sake of simply keeping the body alive but for the purpose of nurturing a healthier one.

When social goals are built on fostering survival, ethical relations prevail and society walks towards self-annihilation. Survival is a condition for self-understanding – plainly enough one has to be alive in order to understand him or herself – but to look for survival as a self-sufficient end, hampers self-understanding and defeats survival. This means that the human struggle for survival has a peculiar characteristic that differentiates it from the struggle of other animals. When people mistakenly think that to survive they must accumulate material and non-material symbols *through* the other, survival itself is at stake. The hindrance comes, again, as a testimony to our unbreakable unity, to the fact that in human beings *even* the search for survival – or the effort to satisfy one's personal desires – cannot be sought individually, using the other as means for this purpose. Desires and needs are collective constructs, made possible by an inalienable reality, and they have to be recognized as such in order to be sought collectively *with* the other.

What development and antidevelopmentist discourses and practices have promised and promoted so far is the possibility of a collective self-satisfaction. This satisfaction in the first discourse is endorsed at the global level. In the latter, as development is criticized, the promise dwells within the borders of the community. Community will be able to promote the self-satisfaction of its members as long as development does not try to impose it from outside. What both sides accomplish, to the extent neither recognizes the requirements of human unity, is to equate development with survival. In either case is development seen or perceived as a process that has to be collectively steered to the achievement of self-understanding.

Through a partial representation of the human condition, development discourse secures the perpetuation of its power, satisfying the self-interest of some, being attacked for not extending these services to all human beings or being demanded to restrict its efforts to its own people and to let others seek, through their own means, self-satisfaction. The best that can be hoped from development or from antidevelopmentist theory and practice is an equal access and perhaps distribution of social symbols, be these locally or globally reproduced and recognized. Both sides take a situation that is already bad and make it worse. They ask for the universalization of the "malignant tumor", for the right of every society to partake in it. Promoting higher degrees of self-realization seems to be outside of their realm of concern, even when they talk about it, disconnected as their discourses are from the recognition of human unity.

So far I reviewed the general characteristics of a relation that acknowledges the condition of human unity and one that does not. Next, I will review the condition of human unity and interdependency in the context of the development's debate articulation of the relation between what has initially been called Third World and First World countries. These relations have been mainly known as relations of dependency on technology, science, money and the ideology of modernity. The sides have been named superiors and inferiors, oppressors and oppressed. The debate has evolved around three supposedly self-evident realities that set the grounds for accusations and justifications of what are meant to be development and alternatives to its theory and practice. These refer, as we saw earlier, to the value-laden nature of human activity and specially an action such as development; to the individual (or community) right to freedom; and to the reality of poverty. As it was also discussed, only freedom would be widely regarded as a common feature of both discourses.[3] Value choices and poverty apparently belong each to

---

3 See Sen (2000) for a well-known discussion of development as freedom.

different sides in the debate and are used as arguments to invalidate each other's position.

None of these three realities are construed from the viewpoint of unity – the condition that makes them possible in the first place, that confers them understandability and, at the same time, can destabilize their social role and authority. The debate, as a result, takes place in a sterile land that, far from having no implications or being neutral in its application, promotes, literally, a struggle for survival: the usurpation of people's wealth, the fight of the oppressor against the oppressed and vice-versa, the depletion of nature. The debate falls distant from its co claimed goals.[4] It does not enhance individual or community freedom, does not reduce poverty, and does not increase the chances of survival. In the best case it substitutes particular tools of oppression by another. It can change social symbols without increasing, however, coherency and fostering personal and collective realization. Since human unity is ignored, new symbols remain as unquestioned as before. They are not answerable to other symbols and cannot consequently be re-appropriated. The cycle of oppression is thus renewed.

Unity and Freedom

Unity redefines freedom, poverty and values and by doing so, as we will see, it redefines the meaning and the purpose of development. Unity moves these realities away from their definition in terms of relations of dependency and independence and places them within relations of interdependence, unleashing thus a power that is capable of promoting ongoing social inclusion and self-realization. Development, defined in these terms, is a worldwide necessity and can only be fulfilled collectively. Development, due to the particular practical transformations of this time and age, can only be a global project, one that includes the peoples of the "developing" and "developed" worlds alike.

As long as some people are perceived as developed and others as underdeveloped, social, political and personal efforts will continue to be directed either towards the alleviation of poverty or towards the purging of development goals and policies from community life and institutions. The consequence will be the perpetuation of peoples' underdevelopment. It is only when we recognize human unity that we realize how underdeveloped the world is and it is only when we relate as one that we develop.

Beginning with the concept of freedom, human unity redefines it as collective self-understanding. Freedom does not release personal choices, nor tries to protect

---

4   See the similarities between anti or postdevelopment authors like Sachs (2007), Colussi (2009), Escobar (2009), Esteva (2009) and those who are, on the other hand, in favor of some type of development, like, Sen (2000), Nussbaum (2001), Johan Galtung (2004), Yunus (2007) and Tortosa (2009).

it, from the weight of others and society. Freedom is not to act as one pleases, as long as such action remains within the limits of the law, cultural traditions or even common sense. The exercise of freedom implies understanding the truth claims that are raised by others (and by oneself). It requires, therefore, an ever current engagement in the mutual validation of social symbols and the shaping of new ones. The more people stay involved in this process the more their capacities are released.

Before I continue with the analysis of freedom, it is important to clarify at this point in what sense I am using the term "capacity", that is, the criteria for identifying the actual exercise of freedom. It can be inferred from what has been said about human realization, as opposed to satisfaction, that not every human action, choice and production represents a human capacity. One's own satisfaction with one's life is not enough guarantee that personal capacities are being released and freedom is expressed therein. The criterion for judging when this process is happening is the realization of everyone else's capacities, that is, when one's actions and choices are actively directed towards this goal. Hence freedom is actualized when one's actions are validated by others as conducive to their self-realization. Here two questions need further explanation, who are these "others" and what is to be validated.

These two questions will be explored in detail in the third part of this book, as I talk about the features of dialogue and the community of universal friendship that it fosters. For now it suffices to say that, as we saw in the previous section, though social symbols may be well established and widely accepted, their reproduction may not lead to self-understanding and realization. Thus again the particular use of this term needs to be clarified. The same problem arises when we inquiry into the "otherness" of one's freedom. The collective process of validation I am referring to has been and still is a practical feature of certain social groups, communities and societies. However, these are still not characterized by freedom, as long as decision-making processes are tied exclusively to membership.

In the development and antidevelopment discourses, freedom is the flight from dependency to independence.[5] From the perspective of unity, freedom is the historical and progressive journey of the human *species* and the cyclical journey of human *societies*, from ignorance of the condition of human interdependence towards awareness of it. From the perspective of the development debate, freedom or independence is an either individual or group accomplishment, not bounded to the way one recognizes others and is recognized by them. From the perspective of unity, freedom is an all-inclusive exercise, it has to symmetrically include all those with whom the person or society initially interacts with and affects. Freedom does not accept double standards.

Furthermore, in its traditional characterization, freedom can be apprehended in the contingency of the time being. It can unexpectedly vanish or be restituted. Because it can, at any given moment, be potentially held from someone by anybody

---

5   See references in footnote 4.

else, the present is its locus. It is in the here and now that the oppressor is made manifest and would have to be coerced into returning the stolen freedom.

From the standpoint of human unity, freedom is not looked for in the present alone. It is within extended periods of time and by means of reasonable inferences about the future – built on present and past historical trends – that one can make use of an alternative criterion to judge and compare how a particular society and its people are faring in terms of freedom. Hence freedom (or the absence of it), like the earlier definition of "capacity", is not a condition that can solely be recognized in the strong will and the self-confidence of present generations. The fact that some social groups see themselves as free or as a matter of fact as oppressed, due to their immediate circumstances, is not enough criteria to conclude that this is indeed the case. It is clear that social movements that struggle for their own emancipation may succeed in moving society as a whole to higher degrees of freedom. However, the use of a historically and normatively expanded criteria of freedom to legitimize such demands for liberation would make such move significantly less violent and reduce social antagonisms in the long run.

The relationship between oppressors and oppressed gains a new dimension when freedom is understood as the characteristic of a normatively united humanity. The oppressor is usually defined as the one who holds other people's freedom in his hands. In this sense, nonetheless, everyone has control over the freedom of others. Due to our unity, once oppression is set in motion, and regardless of who initiated it, everyone becomes everyone else's aggressor, that is, no one is deprived of freedom without also depriving others.[6] Concomitantly, freedom may be given by anyone to everybody else by means of the patterns of recognition that one decides to engage in. It is important to bear in mind that freedom entails both the possibility of choosing such patterns and also applying them in daily relations, which requires reviewing these relations, in this practical process, with all those who claim they are being affected by it. Individuals are free, in a limited usage of the word, to be the initiators of action and interaction. Freedom only expands, however, with the remembrance that whatever direction one decides to go, he is taking many others with him. Freedom, in a more ample sense or the understanding of the meaning of the particular path that one has had the limited "freedom" to choose, is in reality a function of looking carefully at everyone else and honestly asking where they stand in relation to this path.

The seemingly self-evident conclusion that some people have considerably more control over the freedom of others than vice versa only holds true when freedom is interpreted in its limited conception: as a diversification in the possibilities of choice and action. Nonetheless, if there is anything like an inner drive towards

---

6 The fact that one's freedom is jeopardized once he sets the aggression in motion does not imply that everyone's legal condition is one of aggressor. The law evidently does not and should not treat all sides as shareholders of a common responsibility. One of the purposes of practical law is precisely to keep everyone safe from the possible consequences of the normative ignorance of others.

increased coherency and meaning, or self-understanding and realization, then each person deprives the other from what he or she has to say about the other's self-understanding to the same extent that he or she is deprived thereof. Deprivation, as a matter of fact, can only happen at the level of understanding. Material deprivation, as negative as it may sound, must first be interpreted as such by the agent, who, moreover, would only do so in the case that he is unable to attribute a coherent and integrated meaning to it. Thus deprivation refers to the original contributions that each individual and collective self could potentially make to the self-understanding of another but does not. The oppressed are those who do not expand their self-understanding and, as such, whosoever limits the expression of the other's capacities is depriving himself or herself from what these capacities could and would have told them.

The structure of freedom and oppression becomes clearer as we think about the relation between the understanding and the expression of human capacities – a reflection that can only be carried out looking at the life of societies within extended periods of time. As unusual as the assertion echoes nowadays in people's imaginary, a more diversified *expression* of capacities, or an increased diversification of social roles, life styles and social symbols, does *not*, by itself, imply increased freedom. It is the possibility of including these expressions into a coherent framework of action, over an extended period of time, while at the same time answering for them in a consistent manner, what characterizes human freedom. Limiting the expression of one's capacities is not provision enough to hinder freedom nor is increasing such expression sufficient to cultivate freedom.

A reasonable argument about the relation between expression and understanding would be that the more capacities are expressed, the better one can understand them. How does this connection between understanding and expression relate with the equal power people inherently share? Even if one concedes that the power to oppress the process of self-understanding is equally shared, the fact would still remain that the power to restrain and limit one's self-expression is unevenly distributed. But since the exercise of capacities is a fundamental component in understanding them, whosoever is thus deprived, is also not free. Where then would lie the equality of people's power to oppress each other?

As I mentioned earlier, oppression should be understood as the withdrawal of meaning from social action and interaction, and not only as the restriction of action. Though such restriction is an ongoing reality it does not give witness to the inequality of power in the oppression of freedom. The core argument here is that *not* only understanding depends on action but also action is a function of understanding. Communities and peoples known for their aggressive and oppressive behavior may seem to be in a position of advantage, at least temporarily, in regards to the expression of their capacities. It may appear, therefore, that not only their limited freedom of action but also their more complex human freedom is greater than that of those they have been oppressing. This advantage, nevertheless, is an illusion and is doomed to destroy the apparently superior society. To the extent that it refuses to submit its values and skills to the continuous critical judgment and validation of others, it ceases to understand the reason for its actions. When this happens, patterns of social action, thought and behavior enter into a cycle of self-reproduction and self-maintenance. They each attend to their own particular demands for survival, demands that are not committed with social cohesion and coherency and increasingly grow in contradiction.[7]

This self-referential reproduction of social symbols represents oppression, that is, people's dependency on patterns of thought and action that must be reproduced if social recognition is to be granted and self-relation preserved. To the extent that understanding does not grow, incoherencies become fatal, eventually destroying those expressions that the society so eagerly (and violently) protected against the judgment of others. The oppression of the "weaker" in his self-expression eventually leads the "stronger" to incoherent, purposeless and self-defeating expressions.

Concomitantly history is full of successful examples of freedom workers. Those who did not take away power from some to give it to others but who showed people how powerful they were. They showed that power is never *in* one person but always *with* people.[8] Power needs a relation in order to exist. In isolation, no one is powerful. They knew that power does not manifest itself through the restrictions that some one-sidedly impose on others. Because the condition of human existence is its interdependence, power makes itself felt by oppressing the oppressor and also by expanding everyone's freedom, when the expression of someone's capacities are directed to the service of others. No one can make use of power without being captured into the web of unconditional equality – a complex and gradual learning that humanity as a whole renews and grows into.

Freedom workers know, above all, that in existence every being has always to seek to fulfill the sum of its needs in order to attend to any of its particular needs. Human beings have to look for self-understanding in order to guarantee their survival and for human freedom in order to secure their basic animal freedom of action. Freedom workers know that the freedom that some proudly uphold with the cost of other's pain, suffering and degradation, is nothing but the limited freedom of animals, that is, to posses things and hold them without knowledge of cause and hope of another possibility. And the attainment of such self-enclosed end could not be the purpose of a life time dedicated to freedom.

Freedom within the reality of human unity moves away from how it has been portrayed in the development debate. Although the sides would disagree on the meaning and means of freedom, they would agree that freedom is the end that they are seeking.[9] While developmentists see development as a means to freedom,

---

7   Habermas discusses this process as the colonization of the lifeworld by system imperatives as these systems, such as the economy and political systems, are solely committed with their own maintenance. See Habermas (1990b).

8   For a detailed discussion of freedom and human liberation on these terms see Freire (1999) and Boff (2006).

9   Compare the works of Sachs (1992) and Rahnema (1997) with the work of a pro development author like Sachs (2005), for instance.

antidevelopmentists see it as the foe of freedom. Freedom for both sides, however, as we discussed earlier, refers to the same condition of autonomy from the control and dominance of the other – in the case of development discourse it is also from the control of nature. Freedom, in other words, means independence. What the sides in the debate disagree with refers only to the sphere of application of this principle. For one it should prevail at the individual level and for the other it should be a community right.

Freedom, as an expansion in self-understanding, questions the possibility of both: community and individual independence. Efforts to promote development as the maximization of those conditions necessary to the full expression of individual autonomy, or, on the other hand, to promote community's liberation from the forced imposition of Western symbols, reduces the purpose of freedom to survival and fosters collective and individual oppression. Because independence is presented as a possibility, and a highly desired one, it promotes the acquisition and accumulation of symbols without the inclusion of the other in the validation of these symbols. What is looked for in this way is the satisfaction of the need for social recognition, which seems, moreover, to be the only way to individual and collective survival. The effort to achieve such a scanty freedom, however, ends in utter disappointment. People's struggle is deviated from its purpose and survival is threatened.

To put it in another way, freedom as independence does not liberate the oppressed nor eliminate the oppressor. It does not overcome the oppression of the apparent relations of dependency that it initially identifies and intends to abolish. It perpetuates the cycle of oppression as it creates higher levels of unquestioned dependency to social symbols. On the one hand, this freedom is claimed with the purpose of avoiding the influences of Western symbols. Notwithstanding, as the latter is labeled as invalid, at no moment it is asked what they can and have to tell other communities about their local symbols, how would they challenge and review the meaning and value of these symbols. Those who stand in this position try to find ways and arguments to overcome the negative recognition that traditional communities have received from the western world. Among other things, they show how the Third World, global poverty and underdevelopment, are a construction of the West and a recent one. Their task is noble as they try to rebuild a self-image that has been degraded and weakened.[10] They show us how rich in capacities and possibilities non-Western communities are. How the West have been systematically trying to destroy it and how these communities should recover self-confidence in their own ways of life and resist the imposition of Western's symbols. This recovery of confidence in one's capacity, however, is claimed on partially mistaken assumptions and carried out through self-defeating means. Instead of confidence, antidevelopmentists end up recovering for communities and

---

10   See Visvanathan (1991), Gelder (1993), Mies and Shiva (1993), Escobar (2009), Nandy (1997), Quijano (2000) and Fenelon and Hall (2008).

their members the same individualistic and oppressive liberal freedom they are so eager to overcome.

Antidevelopmentists correctly acknowledge the destructive and malignant effects of Western's recognition but they wrongly try to make Western's recognition altogether unnecessary. By showing how much damage it had caused, the antidevelopment discourse concludes that the West, its symbols and its projects, are irrelevant in the process of rebuilding communities self-image. It concludes that this can and has to be an individual process or more precisely a community one. That what the West has to say about other people's ways of life should no longer determine these people's choices. Nonetheless, even if it were possible for communities to protect themselves in this manner, away from the existential gaze of others, such isolation could not foster freedom. And as such, isolationism cannot but lead to destruction.

On the other hand, development claims freedom for all human beings, without distinction of class, race, gender and culture. Leaving aside the gap between what is claimed and what development has actually offered so far (or as a matter of fact, *can* offer), the ideal freedom that justifies the need for development is explained in terms of a universal endowment. Freedom, or the possibility of choosing for oneself the best way of life, can be secured by a particular political system that is consolidated as society thrives economically. In the development discourse, economic growth is rarely justified in its own terms but it is almost always the means to further social and political changes that will ultimately guarantee individual freedom.[11] Politically speaking, developmentists would argue that if individual freedom is to be protected, civil rights along with universal human rights should also be safeguarded.

I do not want to dwell at this moment on the merits of the human rights discourse – which could also be looked at as basic norms of peaceful conviviality and mutual cooperation and not necessarily as a requirement of freedom as independence[12] – but the concept of freedom claimed as a right of the individual poses serious problems. The main and fundamental one, from which other problems arise, is that it assumes the possibility of some individuals and societies achieving development and freedom while others remain underdeveloped and oppressed. As development discourse tries to be generous in its intentions and inclusive in its scope of application, it talks, for instance of the assistance that should be offered to marginalized and excluded communities or segments of society. They concurrently set Western, modern and industrialized societies as the example of free societies that should be followed by others. This does not imply a patent repudiation of other people's culture but instead a call to restitute some missing components that, rather than alter what already exists, will supposedly neutrally fill and overcome some social gaps.

---

11   See, for instance, Sen (2000), Yunus (2007) and Singer (2009).

12   Howard (1995), Habermas (1998), Young (2000), Caney and Jones (2001) and Rodriguez (2004).

The effort to spread individual freedom – no matter how we understand the "real" motivations behind it – creates a collective oppression that can be witnessed in relations within the community and between communities. The idea that some countries have achieved higher degrees of freedom than others because its members can consume more or decide among a greater diversity of life-styles is an illusion. As long as freedom is not a collective and all-inclusive exercise, the so-called "excluded" of the world are a constant witness to the bonds of oppression people in the so-called "free" societies are submitted to.[13]

Whether "developed" countries and its members engage in freedom "operations" and foreign aid for economical, security or moral reasons, for selfish or philanthropic motifs, they never suggest in their words and deed the understanding that their own freedom is a function of the "underdeveloped" freedom. In some cases, the other's "underdevelopment" may be seen as a threat to security and freedom. But interdependency remains at this contingent and reversible level alone. "Developed" nations can at any moment recover their lost freedom which may have been limited, through some immediate threat to their survival, by the "poor" of the world. This recovery may very likely require global and equalitarian measures – an apparently inclusive strategy – but again it is a requirement to avoid the practical threat of the other and not to advance the freedom of both. This is evidenced in the fact that most international interventions do not contemplate possible uses of freedom, once it is "granted" to people.

As a result of this dichotomized way of thinking about "outsiders", Western societies must struggle with the side effects of individualism inside their own house. Freedom is expressed through increased competition and social antagonism as individuals try to escalate the social pyramid of recognition. Social solidarity is forcefully imposed and fragile; mistrust and jealousy are common sentiments; and scapegoating is a socially acceptable practice. Well-being is a function of choosing the right consumption patterns and the fate of others a matter of bad personal choices. No rationally agreed motive is available for why solidarity should not be avoided, when the legal and social possibility do so is contingently present.

Another consequence of the dichotomization of human beings and the doctrine of individualism for developed societies is the likely increase in the indiscriminate production and diversification of social symbols, that is, meaningless social reproduction. Social order legitimizes itself and is maintained in this case through the mechanism of a self-fulfilling prophecy. It presents actualized freedom as the consumption of society's ever more diversified symbols: as diversification grows, it expands the expression of freedom and the freer people are the more diverse their production and plenty their consumption. The fact that people believe that they are "free" to not reason together about their options, to not ask to which extent these options positively contribute and favor the self-realization of all, allows for an ever expanding meaningless social reproduction. This reproduction, I would

---

13   See Boff (1997) for a lucid analysis of the consequences that the so called developed countries must face in this regard.

argue, though stirred by the functional needs of social systems, is only possible due to the human drive to overcoming the void of meaning.[14] Social systems corrupt the expressions of this drive and use them in the benefit of system's maintenance and expansion, but the drive itself cannot be silenced and systems would not thrive without it.

Freedom and Fear

Economic and political systems in modern societies corrupt social action, distancing it from freedom and self-realization. This mechanism of oppression, however, is only possible due to a contingent reality, proper to the so called free societies, that meets with the normative human condition of interdependency. Freedom as independence has infiltrated people's social imaginary and legitimized modern structures and social systems but it has not done away with the intuition that the other, beyond a threat to understanding, is also its only possibility. Under these circumstances, the other becomes unapproachable while still desired and, therefore, potentially more powerful. Social exclusion can only take place as a requirement of system maintenance because the legitimizing discourse of individual freedom turns the ever desired other into a feared threat.

The fear that corrupts social action, reducing freedom to meaningless social reproduction and system's maintenance, reflects the struggle of the self to achieve understanding in a world inhabited by compelling and yet unapproachable beings, whose power for this reason *may* be superior to one's own. As material and non-material means cooperate to keep the "concealment of otherness" in place, the need for association finds itself in a dead end road. Under such circumstances, human vulnerability cannot be voiced; social imaginary and social structures offer no language to translate his persistent drive into a symmetrical and fulfilling interaction. In fear he must hold unto the established order, fearing to lose what he is yet to gain.

The denial that human choices and interventions in the world become valuable *with* the other has a paradoxical (non-intended) effect.[15] Instead of acting towards self-fulfillment, action becomes directed towards the satisfaction of the other. The assertion of independency leads into dependency to those symbols that guarantee social recognition and consequently to the struggle for the acceptance of the other. As we do not associate with one another at a level of interaction that allows for the perception of mutual vulnerability and for a meaningful action, the need for recognition dominates our interactions. Such impoverished level of association, although enacted and actualized, is, nevertheless, felt by the subject as oppressive

---

14   See Habermas (1990b) for an analysis of the relation between system's imperatives and the lifeworld.

15   See also Freire (1999) in this regard.

and unfair, leading him gradually into the depths of a cycle of isolation and dependency that mutually re-enforce each other.

Social isolation, at the individual or collective level, represents the struggle of a vulnerable self to set free from the unknown other who seems to force him into unequal and thus oppressive relations of self-satisfaction. Dependency is the ironic fate of isolation. The more one struggles, the more he feels dependent and the more he will conversely struggle to set free from the other and so on, so forth. This cycle takes place not only because questioning the value of social symbols becomes increasingly more difficult but because it makes the unavoidable influence of the other feel gradually more arbitrary and his power more uneven.

In the so-called free societies fear of the potential uneven power and abuses of the other feeds into the tendency to settle with meaninglessness rather than to risk the little that one got. Hence free societies are very keen of comprehensive laws, norms and regulations, which, tellingly, abound in these societies more than in any other society and at any other time. This tendency carries with it the promise of fulfilling an old age dream, which apparently everyone but the modern man knew it was only a dream: a collective agreement on patterns of recognition that would protect the self against the incursions of others while simultaneously guaranteeing unquestioned recognition and unchallenged "self-realization".[16]

There are manifestly in every society social groups and individuals that mobilize against the dominant social order and its symbols. They are those who, by questioning social conventions, seem to be looking for self-understanding and realization. But again, as long as this process is carried out in exclusive terms, as "one's own way of life", as long as it does not accept the questioning of the other and the possibility of having one's options transformed with him, such reaction is the expression of one's hopelessness in achieving the goal of mutual understanding and the decision, therefore, to settle in with "reality". As old patterns of recognition become too oppressive, not necessarily because they are perceived as a hindrance to self-understanding but because they are not granting *equal* recognition to all, the cry for recognition becomes louder. By not including the other, by not overcoming the fear of his power, the struggle for recognition can promote new patterns of recognition but cannot change the structure of the old relations or the end result of these relations in terms of personal freedom and self-realization.

The antidote to this fear is awareness of human interdependence or knowledge that the other's power is not superior to one's own because reality can only be valued and understood through each other's questions and answers. The other cannot exercise any power over someone who is not in a way connected to him – either by means of valuing the same symbols or sharing a common condition. We cannot feel oppressed by someone who has plenty of something we don't want or are not able to value. Power, therefore, although it may seem to be a personal attribute, is the quality of a relation between beings that only together can

---

16   For a different approach than the one I am taking to the possibilities of recognition in modern societies, see Taylor (1995) and Fraser and Honneth (2003).

accomplish their ends. The role that each subject plays in empowering the relation is irrevocable.

Power is perceived as an uneven endowment whenever the goals of a relationship are set in terms of accumulation alone. As social symbols can be unevenly possessed, some will always appear to grow more powerful than others, regardless of how society tries to institutionalize equality. On the other hand, when the goal is set beyond accumulation and securing equal recognition in order to foster a *meaningful* recognition, power is correctly perceived as the coming together of beings that are inevitably in equal need of each other.

Freedom from the other's power, and from one's own fear of it, lays not in the arbitrary rejection of his symbols or social conventions. Social symbols and conventions may and surely will be reviewed and transformed as people grow in self-understanding. These symbols, however, are the result of relations of interdependency and this is how they should be approached, if the oppression of power is to be overcome. Whatever our wants and needs are, they are the result of relations of recognition that named, shaped and attributed value to them. The path to freedom is based on the full recognition and acceptance of this reality. Freedom is the recovery and assertion of our inalienable role in relations of recognition that determine our self. It is an illusion (and a powerful one) to imagine that we can be alienated from our self through the power of the other.

Unity and Values

The second assumption that unity redefines is that of the value-laden nature of human action, present both in the development and the antidevelopment discourses. Such assumption has supposedly different purposes and justifies different ends in each discourse. Antidevelopmentists use it to justify their demand for a politics of non-intervention and the right of communities to self-determination. This is the case with the argument about the invention and cultural relativity of the development project. Developmentists use the same argument to justify a politics of non-intervention in the domain of the private life of national citizens. Personal choice is a matter of value orientation and preference and as such it should be safeguarded and not necessarily questioned.

The argument about values could still lead us into a third direction that, though opposite to the previous ones, is more coherent with the possible theoretical and practical implications of the argument. It could be sustained that since everything is a matter of value there is nothing intrinsically wrong with the destruction and domination of some value system by another. If there was some reality that could be universally validated then it should be sought and respected. Nonetheless, since human actions are all worth the same and there are no criteria for judging their relative truth, goodness or justice, then whatever happens in the actuality of personal and community relations is just a consequence of the different degrees of material or non-material strength that each value system possesses. Luckily this position finds no sphere of legitimacy in the debate about the value and desirability of development. By leaning on arguments like this, the debate, however, cannot overcome its self-contradictions, even when avoiding carrying it forward to its final consequences.

The defense of the value-laden nature of human activity comes along with an attack to those discourses that raise unequivocal claims to the truth. It is argued that truth claims carry with them a hidden will to power and an intention of domination. However, if truth claims cannot be raised because they cannot be possibly validated, then practical domination would be justified. To be more precise, there would not be anything condemnable with totalitarianism (total control) and the domination of peoples and countries. Actions like this could not even be named domination, as the word carries with it certain assumptions that could not be taken for granted once truth claims are normatively denied. When somebody makes use of an object for personal gratification, the object in this case is not oppressed nor dominated. There are in here no hidden intentions that have to be revealed in order to liberate the object, that is, no pretense truth that has to be downgraded from its claimed status to disempower the subject and empower the object.

Concurrently, if there is nothing intrinsically wrong, bad or unfair with power and domination, that is, a claim against it that could be universally redeemed, then domination would just refer to the unavoidable condition of human interactions. In this case it would be purposeless to say that behind any tale of truth lays a will to power. What would be the purpose of unveiling a "hidden" intention against which there stands no normative criteria that could invalidate it?

In the context of human unity, social values, actualized through social symbols, are truth claims that have been redeemed, in an exclusionist manner, by particular social groups. Their condition differs from those non-contingent realities that make such claims and their redemption a possibility in the first place, such as the drive to self-understanding, the need for mutual recognition and the condition of human unity that the latter determines. Even though truth claims in themselves constitute an inalienable condition of human understanding, their particular content, that is, values systems do not. The individual may choose not to abide to the requirements or carry certain values to its final consequences. Paradoxically, value systems appear to constitute a self-sufficient entity. They give the impression that universal validation is unnecessary and that it is enough for a small group to live by it and to actively protect it against the investing of others, for its status to be safeguarded.

In spite of this, values can and should, however, be questioned, the reasons and interests that sustain them should be unraveled and the truth claims that they more implicitly or explicitly raise redeemed. Through this process, values can be re-appropriated by each person and community to express higher levels of self-understanding. Values become meaningful realities only to the extent that they are collectively and non-coercively questioned. If they don't undergo this all-inclusive process of redemption, if their truth is not asked and they don't get to be a closer expression of those conditions that allowed for their existence in the first place, the right to hold unto one's own values oppresses more than liberate.

The condition of unity places social values in a position where they cannot be used to justify a politics of non-interference – at the collective or individual levels – or to legitimize the domination of weaker value systems by stronger ones. Social values, as the product of the interaction of interdependent subjects in their search for self-understanding, cannot be left to their own device, free to impose their own precepts on people and shape social order. To say that a value system is part of the life of a community, that this community has always been functional and been able to reproduce itself on these values and that, therefore, the same should not be questioned, is to ignore the human condition that makes a social value possible in the first place. Because values are born within interactions that are driven towards mutual understanding, they have to be renewed with every single voice that, directly or indirectly affected by these values, renews itself.

Values are positive and meaningful as long as those who hold and maintain them are aware of their general purpose and are not afraid to search and redeem the truths that they implicitly or explicitly raise. In other words, as long as people are aware that the purpose of their values go beyond guaranteeing social recognition and that they are actually only the means recognition has to promote its end. The realization of this purpose implies that values have to be compared with one another, within the same culture and between cultures. Their diversity cannot be left untouched because of their presupposed equality. This diversity in of itself tells about the possibilities of human capacities and people's mutual need in the realization of these capacities.

The condition of human unity requires that social values be validated even with those that are outside one's community and hold a different set of values. To refuse to do so, to ask what a tradition has to say to another, in the search for mutual understanding and agreement, is to forget that values can be the means for self-realization and limit them instead to self-satisfaction. By not reviewing our values with those who share and those who do not share the same set of values, we destroy their liberating potentiality, turning them into mere instruments of survival.

The same challenge is posed to the argument that since different value systems share an equal status it would be justifiable if the stronger was to destroy the weaker. Because values are not an arbitrary construction, without reason and purpose, because they represent the ways people manifest the richness of their capacities, to overlook what they are able to say to each other would be to reduce human existence to its animal condition.

To overlook the truth claims behind social values is to deny the diversity and wealth of reasons people have to act and interact with each other. The claim that values are either arbitrary constructs or meaningful only within the limits of the community that has created them serves only the purpose of guaranteeing social recognition, that is, self-preservation. Imposing one set of values over another or "respectfully" not questioning their truth, has eventually one and the same consequence: dependency to a reality that imposes itself without reason on beings that fundamentally need to know "why".

Unity and Poverty

Unity finally redefines poverty which, together with its revision of human freedom and values, can redefine our understanding of development. Although the invention of global poverty, and the ways it is used to justify development interventions, is seen as a core problem by antidevelopmentists, poverty in both development and antidevelopment discourses means deprivation of those material and non-material symbols that are valued by a particular community.[17] The main disagreement is not about the definition of poverty but about who or which community has the authority to set the legitimate criteria for identifying poverty. For development planners, such criteria are established according to the standards of Western industrialized societies. In their ambiguous and contradictory discourse about values and freedom, poverty becomes a reality that has to be overcome in order to guarantee freedom, which would the possibility of choosing, free from interference or impositions, one's own individual values. Freedom from the other's imposition – development project – can thus be achieved only after the other has imposed enough to guarantee the maturation of individual freedom.[18]

Nonetheless, if freedom from the other is a possibility only to the extent that one's choices represent value preferences, then development and any other kind of "other directed" project cannot be rationally justified. First of all nothing in the other's preferences could be disqualified so that some kind of "replacement" strategy could be justified. Secondly, it would be a fallacy, from the perspective of the giver, to argue that the other must first hold to certain preferences in order to be able to uphold another set of preferences. If such argument can be made it is because preferences can be ranked and they are not, therefore, simply a matter of arbitrary and irreconcilable preferences. In the case that development project could be justified in one way or another, however, freedom as the possibility of actualizing one's own values and preferences independently of others' choices would be a vain promise and a nonsensical goal.

The critics of development do not overcome this limited understanding of poverty and would agree that poverty refers to lacking those symbols that a community values. The core difference lies in that outsiders should not partake in the validation of community's symbols and thus participate in the definition of poverty. Development critics are not concerned with how poverty itself affects people's self-understanding or with the legitimization of power relations inside communities, that is, with how some people get to be considered inferior and others superior within established social structures. Building on their perception of freedom as a community entitlement, antidevelopmentists' critique goes as far as

---

17   For what would be a "valid" definition of poverty from an antidevelopment perspective, see, for instance, Rahnema (1992), Illich (1992) and Sachs (1993).

18   See, for instance, Sachs (2005). For a survey of different theories of development and their goals see also Peet and Hartwick (1999).

to question which society's standards should be allowed to determine and measure people's different positions within society.

The way beyond this limited understanding of poverty, which gives support to established power relations – instead of being the intended tool for social critique and change – is recovering the condition that makes poverty a possibility in the first place. Poverty, as a local or global reality, is a testimony to our human unity and, at the same time, to the consequences that disrespecting this condition implies. On the one hand, poverty means a certain relationship with the notion of power. It means that power is taken away from its original context within symmetrical relations to be placed on individuals or on their creations. It is only when we forget human interdependence and instead replace it with the possibility of dependency or independence that poverty comes to life. Asymmetrical power relations are in this case maintained through the idea that we are dependent and can consequently achieve independence. When such idea prevails more power is (mistakenly) attributed to those who have accumulated more social symbols, material or not. Holding these social symbols will be the goal of all those who have been deprived of the recognition of being wealthy. The traditional notion of poverty, therefore, is possible when values and symbols are sought after *only* for the recognition that they provide – as if relations of recognition could be unilaterally established or be object directed alone.

To claim freedom, for the community or for the individual, while simultaneously accepting the legitimacy of a particular community or society to determine the content of poverty, at the local or global level, is self-contradictory. There is no freedom in a society where poverty is a possibility of recognition for some, where people have to struggle to meet the standards of "non-poverty" and where social structures are not geared towards the universal re-validation of these standards. Since in the development debate neither community values nor personal values should be subject to collective validation, poverty is a constant possibility and freedom, for this reason, is always under threat.

On the other hand, the invention of poverty is possible because human beings are looking to be recognized in a particular way, that is, because they need one another to know who they are. They are certainly not looking to be recognized as poor but, along with such possibility, come also the hope of being rich and here precisely is where the condition of possibility of poverty rests. The question one should ask is not only what power relations are hidden behind "global poverty" but what is being looked for with the idea of "wealth". The possibility of being socially recognized as wealthy, in any of its forms and content, is the fastest and easiest way to assert one's value and capacity. Hence the idea of poverty not only reflects a misperception about the human condition but it also reflects such condition itself. It tells us about people's mutual need and the purpose of this need. If poverty did not come along with the promise of richness, that is, of a higher and better recognition, poverty would not be understandable. But although the promise of a higher and better recognition constitutes human relations and although social symbols are the substance that gives form to our hopes and relations, we should be careful not to define poverty in terms of these symbols.

Poverty as a standard to measure the accumulation of social symbols will always foster relations of oppression. Getting rid of the "global" in poverty will not bring community's freedom back. Poverty could, however, be a tool for liberation if used to measure the quality of social interactions in terms of the self-realization that it promotes. From this perspective poverty can only be an attribute of the whole and never a trait of some and certainly not a trait of *the other*. Human poverty or limitations in the self-understanding of some affects the self-understanding of all. Poverty, in this sense, is a normatively universal idea which, in the age of globalization, has to be globally overcome, through the efforts of each and every human being.

It is the poverty of humanity that once reduced fosters freedom. In the global age, no society is poor alone, while others are reaching self-realization. To the extent people express their capacities they are contributing to the understanding of *all* others and cannot keep this achievement as a socially enviable trophy. The notion of wealth as that which the human condition seeks to fulfill can move human beings towards relations of moral recognition, where each actively supports the achievement of everyone else. Such notion addresses the question that antidevelopmentalists rightly raise about who has the legitimacy to define poverty and for whom. But contrary to the conclusion that they reach, it is not up to the community alone to validate its symbols. Such decision in no way increases freedom or community's self-determination. It can only make the community subject to its own creations and a slave to the increasingly self-contradictory demands of its symbols.

As people become aware that poverty is not knowing how the capacities of others determine and give meaning to one's own capacities, their efforts to alleviate poverty will be directed towards the collective release of human capacities. They engage in the effort to overcome poverty through the only possible way in this age and time, which is overcoming global poverty. The motivation for this global action is not fear of the other's threats, possible and undesirable immigrations, overpopulation, environmental pressures or violent retaliations. Neither is compassion the main drive behind it. The impulse behind such action is knowledge of human unity and its requirements. In other words, the understanding that in the age of globalization personal freedom and collective self-determination can only be fostered as all the affected by the life style of others are able to participate in an equality of condition – with the same political and civil rights – in the mutual validation of these life styles. Freedom as meaningful realization is gradually actualized as everyone expresses their own choices and capacities at the service of the realization of everyone else's capacities.

In a contingently globalized world, freedom, like the overcoming of poverty, can only be experienced as a global project. Communities evidently try to fulfill their common human need for self-understanding through different means, that is, through the diversity of their social values and symbols. In one community self-understanding and realization may come as its members strive to accumulate material goods, in another as they try to reach higher positions in religious or political structures and so on. Nonetheless, if the members of a community lack the opportunity to engage in the validation of these symbols – if a normatively universal sphere is not materialized within society for this validation – the members will be deprived of the means through which they can understand the meaning of their symbols and exercise their freedom thereof. Conversely, when social symbols can in principle be validated by any other human being, oppression is reversed.

It must be stressed that overcoming oppression and human poverty does not imply necessarily an equal distribution of resources or social symbols, which by every means are irreplaceable instruments in the process of self-understanding and realization. The first can surely affect the latter but such affection is not a function of the *amount* of symbols that has been accumulated. Lack of particular symbols determines specific types of poverty, such as economic, political or spiritual. However, this specific poverty is only socially relevant, that is, meaningful to people's self-relation, in case it affects the possibility of a collective validation of someone's symbols. If the equal distribution of a particular symbol is capable of fostering this process, allowing everyone to re-appropriate old symbols, transform or overcome them and create new ones, then this particular type of inequality or poverty should be overcome for the sake of *everyone*, as it determines *everyone's* poverty.

Different symbols and different patterns of distribution, both at the local and global level, can be validated as to its contributions to the fulfillment of everyone's capacities. If someone's material wealth implies that others cannot develop their capacities, this accumulation should be criticized as a cause of poverty and collective oppression. If, on the contrary, through an all-inclusive actual questioning of people's different levels of accumulation, it is accepted that a particular accumulation favors both the understanding and the expression of *everyone's* potentialities, the differences within a community and between communities are being validated and in no wise can be associated with oppression or exploitation.

It is clear that some types of extreme accumulation are detrimental to people's survival and undermine, consequently, the very first condition for one's self-understanding, which is being alive. As I have explained it earlier, however, one has to be careful not to judge the value of survival according to its own measures and not judge poverty, consequently, in terms of survival. Survival is valuable in and for human beings because it allows for self-understanding. If it were not for what it represents – for the different purposes that it seeks to fulfill in every living creature – the value of human life would be exactly the same as that of any other living being, including the tiniest bugs and plants on earth. We know, nevertheless, almost instinctively, that survival for human beings is not valued as an end in itself. Anyone at any time and in any culture, given that he or she had neither special attachment nor repulsion to a given man or an animal, if having to decide between saving the life of one or another, would choose the first.

In addition to the fact that the purpose of human survival lies beyond itself, survival can also be granted only as its purpose is met. As one grows in self-understanding he is able to survive. This is another reason why poverty should not be measured in terms of survival. A community may be surviving at a particular moment but if it is not promoting growing levels of self-understanding, survival itself is threatened. For this reason to name those who are not able to survive, at a given time, as poor is to direct one's attention to a mistaken source and overlook and ignore the real threat to survival. The fact that millions of people are dying of hunger and starvation, that is, due to avoidable and reversible human threats to survival, cannot be overcome by dealing *directly* with their economic poverty. In the age of globalization this extreme material deprivation is the result of *everyone's* low levels of self-understanding. Likewise, the temporary survival of the so called wealthy cannot be taken as a measure of their success in overcoming poverty. Their survival is temporary, as witnessed by the growing exhaustion of natural resources and increased social tensions and antagonism that accompanies their economic growth.[19] And again, as meaning is not granted by survival, to look for a form of development that can foster survival is to perpetuate the same cycle of a meaningless and endangered survival.

I have explained in this first part of the book that the development debate does not acknowledge the condition of possibility of the claims that it raises on poverty, freedom and the value-laden nature of human action. For this reason, the debate is built on self-contradictory concepts that offer a fragmented perception of the human condition and undermine the possibility of an integrated vision that in the modern age could determine the terms of a more just and equalitarian social order.

The practical result of this lack of normative clarity is the perpetuation of relations of dependency and oppression and the promotion of global underdevelopment. Development and its alternatives are reduced to what poverty, as the absence of Western or local community symbols; freedom, as independence from the interference of other individuals or society; and the value-laden or absolutely relative nature of human activity allow for. Those who criticize development are unable to go beyond this limited understanding and restrict individual and community possibilities to diverse expressions of the same misconceived and misguided actions and interactions.

Development critics, along with those who support development project, perpetuate the power of development and its oppression. Before proceeding with

---

19   It is true that there has been an effort to deal with this "unintended" side effect of modern development project with concepts like "sustainable development" and "appropriate technology" but as antidevelopment authors have shown us – Illich (1980), Visvanathan (1991), Mies and Shiva (1993), Gudynas (2009) – these concepts in no way alter the inherently destructive structure of modern development.

the discussion of how development project can be redefined and understood from the perspective of human interdependence and unity, it is important to ask how development and antidevelopment discourses maintain development's power, influencing and shaping social relations. How are these discourses successful in determining people's self-relation and legitimizing particular social goals if poverty, freedom and values do not reflect people's condition, at least not in the way that the development debate has represented them? What is the normative condition that makes development and antidevelopment power a possibility in the first place?

PART II
Truth and Power in the Development Debate

Introduction to Part II

The fact that the life and self-image of so many people around the world, not to say the majority, have been shaped by the types of action legitimized in the name of development, makes it worth asking and reflecting on the power of development. Why the notions of poverty, freedom and value, have been so successful in affecting people's life and shaping their interactions? What are the claims in these notions that have been indirectly or unintentionally redeemed in order to empower development and antidevelopment discourses?

Before talking about the redeemed claims that development power entails, it would be reasonable to ask whether there is any relation between power and truth. Does power need truth to be maintained? Can one exist without the other? Can we have a powerless truth and a non-truthful power? My argument is that sustaining every power, that is, behind every contingent reality or social structure that endures, there is some non-contingent condition and that the latter is powerful in and of itself. Although the non-contingent expresses itself through material and non-material contingencies and is thus limited by it, every contingent reality also comes to exist and to pass due to the ways it interacts with the non-contingent. In each time and context different aspects of the same non-contingent reality will be expressed as a function of how previous established power understood reality. Depending on what is revealed and what is concealed – which is partially a function of the power structures that are *already* in place but also a function of the particular ways in which these structures *must* redeem reality – a unique interaction between power and truth is generated that influences and determines the course of human action. I will next reflect on the relationship between power and truth as I reflect on those fundamental claims that development and antidevelopment alike must have necessarily already redeemed in order to perpetuate development's power.

Chapter 4
The Truth of Development

The intellectual and cultural movement of the eighteenth century, known as Enlightenment, which eventually contributed to the shaping of the development discourse, corresponds to a well-known effort within Western societies to equate power with truth. The enlightenment thinkers asserted and defended the possibility of a truth endowed with power and condemned pre-modern societies for erecting its power on myths and keeping social order through promises of protection against violent death and satisfaction of easy and simple pleasures. Power had never been before, so they claimed, a function of people's enlightenment.[1] As long as such promises were in place, people would support a ruler and a political regime without regards for any truth claim that may have been implicitly raised by this order. People would, furthermore, stand against those who insisted that these claims ought to be made evident and redeemed.

For ancient philosophers the truth itself is not threatened by power but the unity of power and truth is only one among other possibilities. Political regimes and social life are supported by illusions that are most likely threatened by truth. For these thinkers if power and truth were to coincide a perfect regime would be founded and evils were to cease in the cities. Since this was not the case, however, those who knew the truth had to treat those who had power "most delicately" and subject themselves "to a fierce discipline of detachment from public opinion".[2] In sum, "fortune governs the relations between power and wisdom, which means that men cannot be counted on to consent to the rule of the wise, and the wise are not strong enough to force them to do so".[3]

The Enlightenment finds the ancient way of thinking very timid in its pretensions. It proposes instead that truth and power, that is, the non-contingent and the contingent or the infinite and the finite, come together to establish a social and political order built on human's capacity to make rational choices. Enlightenment's assumption is that humans are endowed with a rational capacity that can apprehend an objective, external and independent reality. Moreover, once the truth is understood, it will be in everyone's benefit to build a social contract

---

1 See Taylor (2007), for instance.
2 Bloom 1987: 284.
3 Bloom 1987: 286.

that respects and fosters this reality. In the age of reason nature and convention can finally come together to serve people's well-being and interests. In the new society, built on science and technology, people can now approach the non-contingent with their own reason and shape the political order accordingly. No longer ostracized for claiming knowledge of truth, scientists as well as politicians are now praised for safeguarding the true interests of humankind.

Although Enlightenment was born in Europe, this way of thinking is not limited therein in its goals and intentions. Holding the responsibility for the world on its own shoulders, enlightenment intended to include each and every society under the scope of its project. Because it refers to universal truths and the universal human capacity to comprehend these truths, it entails a universal project that counts on the particular methodology of universal and mandatory education to enlighten people on how their own interests can be best satisfied through a social order that secures the unity of the non-contingent and the contingent, nature and convention. In few words, through an order where science is discovering the natural world and democracy is fostering patterns of interaction that safeguard and maximize the benefits of scientific discovery for all.

The philosophers of the enlightenment have been criticized for their naïve optimism in regards to the potentiality of human rationality and for their arrogance in believing that social order built on reason would be the most socially just arrangement either for Europeans or for people elsewhere. Questions have been raised about both the potential of reason to determine a universally valid *good* and the willingness of people to live according to the predicaments of reason. Critique has evolved around different aspects of Modernity's unity of the finite and the infinite and, as a result, a diverse set of modern and post-modern social theories and political arrangements have emerged.[4]

In the case of the modern development project, critique has especially evolved around the Western nations' imposition of the modern way of thinking on the peoples' of the world as a means to justify and legitimize their interests of economic and military expansion. In other words, these nations' appeal to supposedly universal ideas, such as human reason and the a-historical and non-relative truth that this reason can apprehend, in order to back up their expansive power.

Critics of development "considered 'reason' to be a historical and regional form of thought rather than a universal potential"[5]:

> It cannot be automatically assumed that modern rationalism is so clearly the
> final, superior form of thought that everyone immediately succumbs to its logical

---

4   See Habermas (1990b) for a detailed analysis of the main theories that have sprung from the critique of Modernity, as Modernity, since its very beginnings, engages in a search for self-assurance. Authors like Bauman (1999) and Horkheimer and Adorno (2000) and deepen in the analysis of reason's unaccounted (and violent) effects for the ordering of society.

5   Peet and Hartwick 1999: 127.

charms, like lost sailors hearing the Sirens' call. Nor should the finest product of rationality, the plenitude of modern life, with its high mass consumption, its ability to match even the most trivial (consumptive) whim, be seen as capable of satisfying all with its seductive, sedative, selfish appeal.[6]

Critics have not only argued that development project, as a project of modernity and enlightenment, has tried to impose its power by unilaterally validating the claimed truth of rational science and modern technology. They have also argued that there is no truth out there to be discovered. If there is no truth for science to discover, the political regime that is in charge of protecting the truth and enlightening or developing people and communities to apprehend it, loses its legitimacy and authority. By destroying the possibility of truth, it is expected that the power that relies on it will recede and competing powers will flourish and settle. A new relation between truth and power is hence established:

> Truth is not outside of power ... as long as we understand by the truth not those true things which are waiting to be discovered but rather the ensemble of rules according to which we distinguish the true from the false, and attach special effects of power to 'the truth'. (Foucault 1980: 131)

Critics of modernity, including antidevelopmentists, reverse the enlightened relation between power and truth. Instead of having the first at the service of the latter they put truth at the service of power. "Culture" is invented as the condition and possibility of knowing and redeeming the truth. The ancient thinker, trying to discover the truth and not being influenced in his discernment by public opinion or the imperatives of his own culture, and the modern thinker, who is blessed to know a truth that has public and political support, are both rejected. There is no nature outside the cave. The cave is all that exists and it creates the truths that are needed for its own maintenance. The ancient philosopher, without pretensions of seeing his truth become powerful, is substituted by the modern philosopher who, living in a fast changing world, sees the opportunity of making the truth the human good and central to ordered life. The post-modern thinkers who follow them invert this relation and have power as the foundation of social order, a power that in its turn creates truths or values to sustain itself.

In many post-modern discourses, however, and this is the case with antidevelopmentist ones, what is sought with this inversion is not necessarily to invalidate science claims to the truth but to weaken the centralized, totalitarian and globalized regime that these claims are associated with. Critics do not find a problem necessarily with the specific content of Western claims, more precisely its rational sciences, but with their relation to power or how they are used to invalidate other truths and to justify domination over non-Western societies' ways of thinking and living. By questioning scientific and rational truths, critics are

---

6   Ibid.

asking "who is this 'we' who knows what is best for the world as a whole?" And since the answer is "the familiar figure of the Western scientist turned manager",[7] science, reason and truth are altogether invalidated. The "tyranny of globalizing discourses" has to be eliminated for a decentralization of power to happen. The alternative to modernity and development is:

> The return of forgotten knowledge, an insurrection of subjugated knowledges, blocs of historical knowledges usually disqualified as inadequate, naïve, mythical, beneath the required level of scientificity. (This task is not) possible unless the tyranny of globalizing discourses (is) first eliminated. (Peet and Hartwick 1999: 131)

To put the truth at the service of power does not imply, however, a decentralization of power. It can also lead to the domination of weaker societies by stronger ones. In spite of the negative reviews that his work has received, I interpret Bloom's (1987) analysis from this perspective. Centralization and social stagnation was the danger that ancient philosophers saw when they went against convention and would not commit their knowledge of the truth. They knew that without this knowledge there would be no hope of change for their societies. It was the existence of a non-contingent reality, independent from society's traditions and habits, which allowed for society to be criticized and higher forms of justice to be sought. The conception of such reality was a constant threat to the established regime and the standard by which social life could be judged.[8] Without this standard or the possibility of knowing it, there is no reason, no justification for why a particular power should not dominate and impose itself over others, that is, no criteria to denounce what is unacceptable with such domination. The absolute relativization of truth, springing from historically weaker social groups, may and most certainly has the intention of demanding a more even distribution of power and fairer social relations – a goal that these groups, moreover, have historically and gradually been successful in achieving. However, the same argument becomes very dangerous in its implications, when and if voiced by stronger social groups.[9] If successful, it would imply even higher concentrations of power.

Unfortunately for the cause of advancing theoretical thinking and political and social alternatives, as the development debate anticipates, the argument for the recognition of the equal value of communities' diverse life-styles and the demand of freedom from Western's totalitarian power, places both sides of the debate under the same enlightened discourse of development. The debate over development has been entangled in a set of conceptual contradictions and legitimized over and over the same oppressive power structures. By rejecting the possibility of a non-contingent reality, antidevelopmentists have not strengthened community's power

---

7   Escobar 1995: 193.

8   Bloom 1987.

9   In this regard, see the elucidating analysis of Appiah (2005).

nor weakened Enlightenment's project. They have just given new expressions to arbitrary power, supposedly freed from the bonds of normative demands but conversely sustained on partial and fragmented claims to the truth.

To understand why the antidevelopment discourse does not overcome the theoretical and practical difficulties that they identify in the development discourse, we must first ask ourselves how were the enlightened thinkers conceiving the truth when they saw the possibility of building a political order that reflected the truth or that was validated by the truth it behold.

Enlightened Self-interest

Enlightenment thinkers, unlike ancient philosophers or the prophets of the later "postaxial religions",[10] were not referring to those things that human beings *ought to* do so that their actions would reflect the beautiful, the just or the good. They were instead referring to human passions and drives, to those things that human beings *do* and are inclined to do, away from the requirement of self-denial.[11] When they referred to the human condition and the purpose of social life, they appealed to utilitarian goals, centered in the interests of the individual and "directed to ordinary human flourishing" (Taylor 2004: 65). If social control and discipline were required to fulfill this very ordinary and mundane end it was only temporary and with the purpose of "promoting self-discipline" (Taylor 2004: 44) – not as an inherent requirement of a higher or transcendent way of life. It was on this basis that the first, though not the later, thinkers of modernity asserted that from then on power could be at the service of truth.

Modernity had to reduce the human condition and the reality of truth itself to make truth and power coincide. Until now the truth was not available to all and almost no one had a practical interest in it. Just a few would care to know it; fewer yet would know it and almost no one could abide by its precepts and live accordingly. Thanks to this reduction "the people, who were by definition uneducated and the sear of prejudice, [can] be educated, if the meaning of education [is] changed … to enlightened self-interest."[12] Enlightened self-interest is what makes it possible for people to support and to obey civil authority and the rule of law.

For pre-modern societies, self-interest and the common good, or that which is true and just for everyone, were irreconcilable. To establish an ordered society that was based on truth, and thus just, people had to sacrifice their self-interest in favor of the common good. They had to become virtuous. But they could not, that is, they could not freely give up their personal good for the common one. A cohesive social order had to be kept, therefore, through "divine commandment and

---

10   See Taylor (2004), chapter 4.
11   See Taylor (2004).
12   Bloom 1987: 288.

by attachments akin to the blood ties that constitute the family",[13] that is, through fear of God's wrath and by appeal to other immediate and more instinctive feelings and emotions.

The distinction that modern thinkers establish between self-interest and "enlightened self-interest" points to the possibility of a political order that can have the non-coercive consent of all its subjects. This is a consent that does not repress people's selfish interests but grows precisely as people actively seek to foster and protect them. Making use of their rational faculty – now reduced to instrumental-utilitarian rationality – people find out that their ordinary interests of prosperity and long life can actually benefit from a particular type of social contract.

The problem that arises from a relation between the now unashamedly selfish individuals that can freely choose the type of social contract they want to engage in is that the substance of this contract or the common good has to be significantly reduced. The common good, that is, the possibility of a universally validated reality, is reduced to the preservation of the self, against violent death or the exploitation of others. When the common good is thus defined, it is clear how political order can then be consensually maintained. Everyone, virtuous or not, can understand that a social contract whose only purpose is to protect everyone against the advances of others is also desirable from a personal point of view. Unfortunately for the fate of modern societies, this negative role is all that is required from its political order, its institutions and laws and everything that is public.

The source of power in modern societies is this reduced truth, manifest in scientific rationality and its technological products. These do not ask people to grow closer to any particular ideal reality nor to control their instincts and primitive emotions. Commerce, as the so promised civilizing activity of Modernity, only substitutes violent passions by more polite and tamed ones. In no ways it opposes self-centeredness to an ordered society. In non-modern societies people's selfishness could not unite them under a cohesive order. The first, therefore, had to be relatively controlled and submitted to the requirements of the latter. Although this did not translate into a more peaceful society – medieval European societies were internally more violent than modern ones – life in community required accepting duties, sacrificing self-love for the love of others and controlling one's inclinations. It is only in the modern world that this hierarchy finds grounds to be legitimately reversed. People no longer have to accept difficult duties or go against their newly invented "inner" self to be welcomed into an order that, in the older times, could at best promise to carry forward the risky task of pleasing unknown deities.

In modern societies, people can give full expression to their inner self and demand and expect that it be respected. The language through which this now legitimate expectation finds expression is that of individual or private rights, as opposed to public. The public – now differentiated from the personal – is deprived of a self-referential existence and justified on the protection that it grants to

---

13   Bloom 1987: 167.

individual rights. And the means that it has to pursue this end is the promotion of science and technology. Modern political power deals with an entity – nature – that, unlike the unpredictable will of ancient gods, can be dominated by scientific rationality and controlled by modern technology. From the acknowledgement of a human condition that fears death and strives for self-preservation, follows the argument for a social order and a political power built around the truths that scientific rationality alone can reveal and turn into an instrument for the preservation of all.

These initially local changes were envisioned to become a universal project, one that would be embraced or, if necessary, imposed on all societies as the advantages of being ruled by a political order that would reconcile the newly differentiated private and public spheres, became self-evident. What was not mentioned as this project was carried throughout the world is that to enjoy the fruits of this rational and non-coercive order there was a price to be paid. One could benefit from all the advantages of reason turned instrumental-utilitarian-purpose oriented, and have everyone else's work cohere into one's own benefit, if he was willing to let go once and for all of the old dream of understanding the truth, collectively validating it and living accordingly. The society that puts power at the service of truth is one that minimizes human interest to only what scientific reason is capable of providing: survival.

When human condition is reduced to the means and possibilities of scientific methodology, the political order, more than fostering human and collective potentialities seeks to protect private individual rights. In other words, by giving up other possible *collective* dimensions and aspirations of their condition, human beings gain the right to pursue personal interests. The discourse of private rights embodies at its core the idea that life together can be so organized that everybody will therein gain as long as all seek to satisfy their own interests. Private rights, as the freedom to do as one pleases as long as it does not interfere with the same right of others, cannot in principle involve any *collective* action – since the other would necessarily impose limitations upon one's own decision of what "pleasant" or "good" is. Under these circumstances, when people are not compelled to review the content of their interests together, the most that they can achieve collectively is self-preservation. Modern thinkers hoped that people everywhere, rational and fearful of death as they all were, would consent to abide by the kind of society that, under the banner of individual rights, would bring together the power and the truth of self-interest. In Bloom's words:

> The nations must all gradually become similar. They must respect the rights of man. ... In fact rights are nothing other than the fundamental passions, experienced by all men, to which the new science appeals and which it emancipates from the constraints imposed on them by specious reasoning and fear of divine punishment. These passions are what science can serve. If these passions, given by nature, are what men have permission – a "right" – to seek satisfaction for, the partnership of science and society is formed. Civil society then sets as its sole goal that satisfaction – life, liberty and the pursuit of property

– and men consent to obey the civil authority because it reflects their wants. Government becomes more solid and surer, now based on passions rather than virtue, rights rather than duties. (1987: 287)

This is in very broad terms the picture of modernity's project and the source from where development theory and practice will spring. Within this context it is easy to understand why development is most commonly defined as achievements in freedom. This freedom is understood in two complementary senses: a) freedom from the constraints of nature, which is fostered through the progress of scientific knowledge and b) freedom to pursue one's own interests, which is best fostered by a (capitalist) democratic order.[14]

The development project is the apex of the enlightenment thinkers daring step to unite power and truth. Development reduces truth to global poverty and the human condition to the desire to overcome it. By looking at human reality from this narrow perspective, development can make the alleviation of individual poverty coincide with the interest of the collectivity, or the common good. It will finally justify the need for a power based on science, technology and free market economy – the only power that can keep selfish and wealth driven individuals together within an economically prosperous society.

Building on the first enlightenment assumption that all human beings seek self-preservation, development goes on to identify those conditions that threaten preservation, gathering them under the general design of poverty. The alleviation of poverty becomes synonymous with enlightened self-interest and, as everyone seeks to overcome poverty, a global power is formed and maintained. Because poor people everywhere are faced with the same undesirable conditions, the particular power that guarantees everyone the right to overcome such conditions feels entitled to raise claims of universal validity. A global society, conceived on these terms, is legitimate to the extent that it alleviates its members from unnecessary restrains. For this reason the standard of development for any society is success in reducing such restrains, that is, in fostering freedom from nature and other people alike. By creating the problem of global poverty, development justifies a global society built on science, technology and individual rights.

It is important to note that development theory and practice are not trying to enlighten people about their interests. It is looking to enlighten people about their *self*-interest – which is first and foremost the desire to overcome poverty and to survive – and to contribute to a social and political order that can foster this goal at the collective and individual level. As long as people everywhere accept that this is their true condition and the truth they are looking for, there will be indeed no better example to follow than the one set by the Western, industrialized and developed societies.

---

14   See United Nations (1951), Peet and Hartwick (1999), Sen (2000), Roberts and Hite (2000) and Nussbaum (2001).

One could say that in the global political regime development predicates, the nations that are already developed have a special place. They are the fulfillment of the dream and the bearers of the promise that everyone everywhere will have the power to actualize or redeem the truth. Through the use of scientific-instrumental reason, made possible by universal education, the peoples of the world will realize how detrimental to their self-interest poverty is and how a society shaped on the standards of development can alleviate this poverty. Once education awakens people's reason to these needs and rights that they have but have remained neglected or unattended by their own communities, protecting, looking up and imitating developed societies becomes crucial for self-redemption.

Next, I will recover the effort of antidevelopmentists to undermine development's claim to the truth and explain why instead of weakening development's power, they consolidate it, by further validating its truths.

Antidevelopment Critique to Development's Truth

By criticizing development in particular and modernity in general, anti-developmentists intend to overcome the main reductions development theory incurs and the oppressive relations that its practice sustains. The central object of critique has been development's claim that there are some truths and that a privileged access to these is available through the combined means of scientific rationality and a politics geared towards the protection of private and individual rights. If it can be shown that such claims are pointless because truth, as a universally valid claim, is not a possibility but a mere instrument at the hands of power, then the power of the development project and that of the developed nations to determine the terms of the relations between nations will be severely threatened.

"Truths are illusions we have forgotten are illusions"[15] and although they are fundamental for the existence of cultures, they do not hold a universal status and do not refer to a reality that can be discovered or agreed on. Truths are the mutually contradicting inventions of power interests. The core problem with development, therefore, does not rest in the content of its truth, which may be adequate to the perpetuation of Western societies' interests. What cannot be accepted is development's pretension of knowing the sole and only truth, its insistence that knowledge of reality can be ranked and that its own truths do not need to accept and coexist with another's. It is expected that as a result of this realization, the scope of development power will be gradually reduced from a global to local level as the non-developed are empowered against development. If development could restrain itself from becoming a global project or if those social structures determined and committed with scientific rationality and individual rights could be local arrangements alone, development, modernization and the enlightened way of thinking would be able to hold their relative truth.

---

15 Nietzsche 1976: 84.

If the development project was to remain within the boundaries of its own birthplace there would not be in the antidevelopment discourse any grounds to denounce development's conception of human beings, enlightened self-interest and how the political and social order is to deal with the tension between self-interest and the interest of the others. Antidevelopmentists have nothing to say about the West's historical choice to view the world in a particular way, that is, about the consequences for the Western people themselves of embarking in the endeavor to unite power and truth. They have nothing to say about the value of science, of reason, of human rights, of technology and the fear of death, as long as the value of these ideas is not imposed on other communities. It is not the truth claims of these traits that are under surveillance but the fact these claims invalidate the *possibility* of other claims.

The lack of concern with the validation of Western's way of life owes to the fact that theirs is just one among many other possibilities. No common standards are accepted, no privileged position granted from which these possibilities could be compared and assessed. Since each community can only talk about its own preferences, critique of the substance of the other's way of life is purposeless. From this initial assumption, antidevelopmentists conclude that relative community truths, that is, preferences, have the right to co-exist peacefully with each other. It is the *right* of Western people to live the way they do, no matter how wrong, unfair or ugly it may look for other people, and this right should be respected if others are to hold the same right.

Building their critique in this way, antidevelopmentists miss the point. They miss the opportunity to propose a real alternative to development. They neither correctly identify the problem of development nor present alternatives to face the threats that development project poses to people everywhere. They end up reproducing the same pattern of thought and using the same set of arguments that development uses to justify itself. Consequently, the discourse not only falls short in unraveling the contradictions of development project but it unintentionally gives support to its theory and practice. It systematizes a rationale that legitimizes development power and invalidates those claims that would weaken it. The novelty of the antidevelopment discourse is to transfer the borrowed set of arguments to a different social setting, moving it away from the relation between individuals towards the relationship between societies and social groups.

What the critics should do, as they try to undermine the power of development, is to inquire into the content of development's truth and, consequently, the foundations on which its power is built. It is only logical that since the possibility of a universal agreement on truth is being questioned, attention will not be paid to the content of truth claims but only to the contingent effect of such claims, that is, the relations of power that it authorizes. However, to overlook the fact that power is intimately dependent on what is being determined as the truth may unintentionally take us back to the assertion of the same truths. In fact the development departs from the truth of survival to arrive at the relativity of truth, while the antidevelopment discourse departs from the relativity of truth to arrive at the truth of survival. None of them believe in the possibility of an agreement that transcends the most immediate and contingent reality and both end up entangled in the concept of power as the all-encompassing reality that determines every other truth.

Modernity brings truth and power together as social order is legitimized on claims that can be validated by all social members. This new basis for the legitimization of authority is not only due to changes in the material circumstances of life, which allows for the factual universalization of participation, but also, as we just saw, due to a reductionist twist on truth and the claims that are put forward for public validation. The notion of truth did not use to refer to knowledge of those conditions and requirements of ordinary flourishing alone. It included knowledge of the good, the beautiful and the just. Knowledge of those realities valued by themselves and not as a means for the purposes of survival or self-preservation. Pre-modern social order could not claim that the basis of its authority was the maximization of personal interest because what was good for the whole – or beautiful and just – was not accessible for personal validation, or collective, as a matter of fact.

In modern times people are more aware of the tension between self-interest and collective interest, due to the widely accepted principle of individual freedom, but simultaneously freer from its demands, because social order builds its legitimacy on the basis of truth claims that can be redeemed here and now. While for pre-modern societies truth and power would either come together in the afterworld or on the day of the Final Judgment, with the reduction of truth to survival matters and true-self to self-interest, society can claim that its truths are universally redeemable, if someone is to take an interest in redeeming them, and make self-interest thus coincide with the common good.

The spread of modern science and technology has also been instrumental in supporting the modern contingent unity of power and truth. Science, as a the use of reason towards utilitarian results, is not only the actualization of a particular notion of truth but it also functions as a bridge between individual interests and the common good. They enable society to direct its structures and institutions towards the maximization of self-interest, that is, to conduct its affairs on the basis of common criteria for the evaluation of advances in both collective and individual well-being. What can be correctly criticized in this process is that the application of a single measure by the political order to validate its authority in regards to the social cohesion and individual benefit that it grants reduces the likelihood of people actually mobilizing and engaging in the validation of the claims that are publicly raised.

The critique of the coming together of power and truth by antidevelopmentists ends up supporting the same reductionist twist that Modernity commits and perpetuating the same unquestioned power structures. Unlike pre-moderns who, in the exercise of power, were unrestrained by truth claims that could and should be collectively validated, antidevelopmentists demand that more powerful nations do restrain themselves. Unlike moderns, however, they argue that this restrain cannot be built on universilizable claims. The result of this discursive effort to set free from oppressive alien power, without recourse to universal agreement, is the validation of local power structures. Because this power, however, should not expand arbitrarily, it is necessarily sensible to some type of claim, that is, answerable to particular demands.

When a self-limiting expectation is imposed on power, a non-contingent reality is brought into the equation. If, however, the requirement to limit power is not placed on truth because the possibility of universal agreement has already been ruled out, the power limiting truth is reduced to a basic common denominator: the pre-existing agreements that make power structures understandable and acceptable. The limitation of truth to claims that have already been validated or, on the other hand, to claims that can be validated without an actual universal participation, serves the same general purpose which is the preservation of these claims and the legitimacy that they grant to the established order. Paradoxically, nonetheless, when self-preservation is the final order of the day, power becomes responsible to almost nothing, answerable only to a stronger power, and defeating the goal of self-restrain.

This is the reason why the development project has gone unchallenged. Since its power is only answerable to claims of self-preservation and survival, the antidevelopmentist struggle to contain it by invalidating the possibility of universal agreement, does not tackle the source of oppression and, inadvertently, supports the same power structures that are already in place. As long as this reduction is not challenged, society will lack alternative references to validate the common good. Power is hence set free, not because people are not able to validate truth claims and reach a common agreement but because some truth claims are already so evident that they do not need to be validated anymore.

Chapter 5
Overcoming the Power of Development

Development discourse and policies have been flourishing everywhere for at least the last 60 years. Although these policies have never been successful in the actualization of development's goals, that is, the promotion of increased socio-economic equality and as a result global security, in fact all data and analysis give witness to the opposite,[1] it remains, nevertheless a triumphant *project*. From the perspective of its core tenets and goals, development has not changed. Development strategies and methods have continuously been reviewed so that development goals are more effectively met but the goal of development itself remains untouched, faithful to the original purpose of development. The growing range of development, like the broader process of modernization, remains so unchallenged, in spite of widespread opposition, that every type of effort that touches upon the object of development (poverty) has been subsumed to the logic of development. The practices of charity and international aid, for instance, are increasingly looked upon as *ineffective* and "free market" alternatives are sought to replace it.[2] Such an approach is only possible and understandable if development standards and truth claims are taken for granted, that is, if they have been gradually validated.

The fact that the power of development remains unchallenged leads us to question the sources of this power. A particular power may well be sustained by a stronger power and beneath all of them may be nothing but a mere contingent twist in human's fate. However, as long as the effort to overcome power is carried on *discursively*, it is the discursive claims on which power is built that have to be undermined. By invalidating the truth, critics of development not only pursue the same contracted reality that development discourse and power validate but they also commit an internal contradiction and fail to explain why development power should not strive to become global.

The power of development cannot be overcome without an understanding and engagement in the validation of the truth claims that sustain it. With this purpose in mind, a task which we have already initiated in the first part of this book, it would

---

1 For a comprehensive analysis of the growing global inequalities and threats to the environment see Held and Kaya (2007) and Lambin (2007) respectively.

2 This discourse is especially evident in the analysis of development strategies in the African continent. See Calderisi (2006), for instance.

be reasonable to argue that modern power is ultimately unconceivable without the idea of people's "rights". In its turn, the right to pursue one's personal or collective end is – in the absence of the possibility of knowing anything better, fairer or more beautiful – the right to pursue those ends that the established power has allowed for – that is, material wealth, freedom as non-interference and personal preferences. This does not mean necessarily that local or national powers have always the last word, as it is clear with the growing prevalence of counter-tendencies such as the human rights movements and policies of humanitarian intervention. But when the claims raised either by local powers or by global scale organizations are not questioned and validated, the stronger power will re-enforce self-serving realities and outlaw threatening ones.

I will next inquire into the idea of rights as manifest in development and antidevelopment discourses. Endowing people with individual rights both sides undermine the condition for a collective search for truth and the transformation of the prevailing structure of power relations. No claim beyond self-interest is redeemable enough to constitute the basis of power structures, particularly as it determines the relation between different peoples and societies.

Following this discussion, I will recover my initial reflections on peoples' search for self-understanding to explain how awareness of an expanded human condition weakens the power of development as it releases the power of a renewed normative understanding.

Modern Individual Rights

Rights, in the modern world, refer to the possibility of seeking one's well-being in tandem with everyone else. They are both an attribute of free individuals and the means for the actualization of freedom. They also imply reciprocity as mutual respect, which sets the requirement for the equal protection of everyone's rights. Universal reciprocity, however, is not justified in normative terms, as a fundamental mutual need. The implication of this characterization of rights is that every choice should be equally respected not for some inherent reason or valuable condition that it may embody but for not representing a threat to other people's choices. This negative validation of individual rights applies both to individual and collective choices.

Collective choices can and are questioned by individual members, both in more or less modern societies. In modern free societies, however, such questioning has paradoxically led to an increase in the numbers of laws, norms and regulations. The factual growth and demand for these regulations are the result of a questioning that is not directed to the value of people's choices. Questions are asked only about the choices' "hindrance" aspect and within power structures that determine that only those choices that hinder others' can be legitimately questioned. As such, social regulations are ever more needed to police the borders between individual choices which, prevented from understanding each other's mutual affect, must be forcefully kept away from the sphere of each other's influence.

There are social spheres where people can look upon group choices and validate them together. As long as these choices, however, are accountable only to group members and outsiders cannot legitimately question them because to do so would be a threat to the group's or community's right of choice, choices are again the manifestation of particular power structures more than the group's right to make unique and valuable choices.

When social structures and institutions do not contemplate universal participation in the validation of individual and collective choices, the value of one's choices become subject to what power structures allow to be reproduced. Thus someone may advise his son to become a doctor or a supervisor demand that his employee do not work under the effect of alcohol, but if the social value of these actions is not practically redeemed through an all-inclusive process, becoming a doctor or not drinking is responding to system requirements more than the expression of one's choice or an originally conceived purpose.

The practical result of the discourse of individual rights is the reproduction of actions which – detached from the possibility of a universally redeemable social value – require a growing number of laws to regulate their mutual interaction. Ironically, freedom of choice is gradually retracted into abidance to laws. In a society that stands on the principle of individual rights, lack of actual validation leads to arbitrariness of choice and the latter to increase regulatory constrains – the mechanism that uninformed choice has to keep the semblance of freedom.

The same problem arises at the community level and in the interaction between communities. When only insiders are allowed to validate internal choices, without concern for how these choices not only deprive other people from the same exercise but, more importantly, how they can contribute to the self-understanding and fulfillment of others, the "common good" become in need of increase regulation in its interaction with the common good, or the national interest, of others. And, in the case that international norms and regulations do not expand fast enough, the right of the nations to pursue their own interests is the practical right to pursue those ends that the most powerful has determined as so.

For this reason not only the freedom that individual rights promise to protect but also the reciprocity that it supposedly implies is a practical impossibility. The right to maximize one's interests requires a growing number of laws to steadily regiment people's choices and interactions, leading to a self-contradictory reciprocity. The problem is not that of simply finding the right balance between freedom and equality. Respect to the social and personal value of "individual rights" is questionable because it stands on a notion of freedom that excludes from its materialization the universalization of individual choice. As such one does not need and is actually held back by the other. The effort to promote equal respect in the international scenario to individualistically conceived freedom – though collectively, that is, nationally claimed – overlooks the fact that the first cannot promote the latter and the latter will always undermine the first.

Contrary to commonly held argument, development project can do anything its power allows for in the absence of universalizable truths. The detection of a common interest in self-preservation, that is, a common instinct that people everywhere would share, has nothing to do with the discovery of a common humanity, as antidevelopmentists like to put it when criticizing the abuses of development. More than a common humanity, development has "discovered" our shared animality, a condition that, moreover, not even the most pre-historic societies would disagree with. It is this "discovery" that allows development to expand its power over the world, in every community and at every home, imposing itself as the desired good of all.

The modern discourse of individual rights, on which development project relies to legitimize its power, and on which the antidevelopment discourse builds its social critique, ignores the social and universal basis of choice. Because one's choices and preferences are not determined alone but in society, inside relations of recognition, the ends that one has the right to seek are enabled by and within societal structures. The social shaping of individual choice does not mean, however, that people cannot value and choose their own original ends. This apparently social constraint is also the condition of understanding the meaning and the value of choices. As we ask each other about the meaning of our choices or the reasons for willing and doing what we do, choices are re-appropriated, that is, social goals are turned into one's own.

But in addition to being a social process, freedom to decide about one's goals and well-being is also an all-inclusive process. The re-appropriation of social symbols requires asking what *any* other has to say about our capacities and telling him, with our respective choice to display one capacity or another, of his capacities. As we question together the reasons for acting and expressing one set of capacities over another, continuously redirecting our actions towards the maximization of everyone's capacities, we are engaged in a universal relation that is fostering self-understanding and moving away from self-preservation. The effort to protect individual private rights, to keep the other away from one's decisions or to restrict the decision-making process to members alone, is to commit the search for one's true self or freedom to the reproduction and preservation of those best established social goals and symbols. Freedom, as the possibility of understanding the social value of one's choices, has to be continuously actualized within relations that include anyone who has something to say about these choices, in regards, moreover, to any of its aspects, not only its negative "hindrance" effects. Outside interactions of this nature, the right of the individual to choose his goals and pursue his interests does not represent the fulfillment of the individual's original and unique self but the reproduction of systems' requirements or social traditions and customs.

As long as the requirements of preservation are locally contained and do not affect other people's choices, the above mentioned contradictions and paradoxes will not be manifest and the necessity to overcome them will not be felt. However, as soon as this trend is overcome, particularly through expansion and conquest, colonization and more recently globalization, the effects of a power set loose from universal normative obligations are made visible everywhere. "Respect to the other's rights", a modern moral code that apparently may control the reach and effects of power, implies only respect to the other's power. Its actualization results, in the best case, in a balance of power and, if such balance is not possible, in the spread of one's rights and interests over others. The side "respected" as the more powerful – and not the one who have had its choices questioned and eventually validated – is the one who determines what "legitimate defense" is and what is "barbaric terrorism"; what "genocide" is and what is "protection of human rights". When rights replace truth, the difference between the former is not the validated reality that each entails. Their difference rests on *whose* rights have been offended and which power was eventually successful to define them as so.

If truth claims implied in personal and collective choices cannot be possibly redeemed in regards to the value of these choices to everyone's self-understanding, "the right to do as one pleases as long as the right of others is not hindered" will not protect local communities from the West's exercise of its rights. As a matter of fact, it will (as it has) engage all in a struggle against all. Within this logic both sides agree that what exists is just their relative truths or non-commensurable choices and both assert their right to express and pursue them. As such, both become subject only to the traditions they profess or to the power that maintains these traditions. Without any other criteria to recognize and legitimize a right but the existence of a collectivity that professes it, "respect to the other's right" is a function of the power of the collectivity that asserts and seeks respect to its rights. In the absence of either a practical balance of power or a normative agreement on redeemable claims, the fate of people is sealed by the power structures that each particular value system requires for its maintenance.

What Can Limit Power?

When disagreements arise about the limits of the other's right, which is the question involved when a power is identified as superior and abusive or threatening, negotiation, mutual tolerance or respect to the other's rights or borders will not solve the tension. These are useful tools only when there is a perceived balance of power and the maxim of "mutual respect" can thus prevail as a self-sufficient and self-explanatory regulatory norm. When the power and thus the right of the other are not acknowledged, disagreements will be resolved through exploitation, invasion, or the use of direct violence – which will receive the most diverse names, from holy war to freedom operation or global development. What could limit power in a non-violent and non-threatening way is not, as antidevelopmentists mistakenly assume, the nonexistence of truth but precisely its possibility. Only if truth claims are redeemable, power representations can be held accountable.

Discourse cannot put an effective halt on power, including the power of development, if it paradoxically denies the condition of discourse itself, that is, the condition of mutual understanding. When those ends that people have the right to pursue cannot be collectively and universally questioned and validated, when their relative goodness cannot be valued and assessed and, therefore, transformed, there remains only the *preservation* of people's choices through the literal elimination of adversarial power.

If this is the path to the assertion of one's rights, nonetheless, there is no room for writing and creative discourse to justify certain actions, delegitimize others and demand social change. There is only wishing good luck to those engaged in the battlefield of power. But as long as the first path is being taken, as long as there is public debate about alternatives to social action, there is an evident appeal to truth, to agreement on a reality that can be universally redeemed, even if such appeal is at first sight not as well-structured and evident as it had to be.

If a non-contingent reality can exist away of contingent power structures and relations, there stands a normative horizon to correct the abuses of power, and thus a ground for criticizing development theory and practice as oppressive and overcoming the power structures that it sets. Nevertheless, if such an independent criteria that is not corrupted by power exists, it has to be collectively sought, validated and agreed on. Truth is not necessarily represented in the values and symbols of a particular community. It is not represented by what is best for each community alone but what is best for all. Because what is best for all is far from clear and, in the age of individual freedom, anyone can in principle demand that what has been pre-determined as good be reviewed, truth needs to be continuously sought after and its content needs to be defined inside this actual search. Thus the academically oriented effort to determine normative criteria for the critique of development's theory and practice can only be coherent with the condition of truth if it asks about the general structure of this search, more than about the substantial content of truth.

To say that truth has to be sought is to say that conceptual inconsistencies and contradictions in social practice have to be looked for, identified, and a temporary agreement established on the most coherent course of action at a given moment. As such, the truth has to be sought not only inside community boundaries but also through the coordinated effort of communities as they work together to decide how to solve a given problem of mutual concern.

Agreement, as a matter of fact, is sought over power representations, through an all-inclusive process that is accountable, before everything else, to the principle of universal *positive* reciprocity. If the power of development is to be overcome by a different power structure, the values and symbols of every social group and individual, that is, every claim that gives legitimacy to power structures, has to be universally validated. These claims are called into question regardless of whether the power they support is hindering the power of another (external) social group or not. They are questioned in regards to their mutual coherency and for the advancement of mutual understanding.

Life styles cannot be *a priori* validated, as the result of the good will of the powerful or the fear of the weak. Social and cultural differences in interpretation that give rise to theoretical and practical disagreements can only be validated *in* the process of asking what each has to say about the perceptions of the other. World views and their respective power representations have to be approved by everyone as conducive to the self-understanding and realization of all and each *person*.

Such approach is different from the current antidevelopment critique of development. Development and modernity should be criticized not only on the assumption that in the world there should be room for diversity and differences but also on the premise that each of these differences – as a group *and* as an individuated person – has something very specific to say to and about the other. If the practical power of the modern way of thinking and scientific rationality are to be eventually limited and transformed it is not simply because there are people in the world who hold different values but because these differences have not yet redeemed the truth of these modern expressions.

When social critique is built on the principle of substantial redemption, demands are not placed on power for overcoming disagreements. Although agreement is looked for at the level of action, it is not at this level that agreements are validated. Any practical disagreement will have to be *normatively* considered and the claims therein carefully attended as the sides engage in the search for truth. In this search power structures and relations are challenged and eventually replaced. This replacement is fundamentally distinct from the one that results from a confrontation of powers where the stronger destroys the weaker, either by the use of direct force or by unilaterally spreading the desirability and need for its own values. As partial and incomplete perceptions of reality come across each other, societies can review their well-established values under the light of a new understanding. They undergo a transformation in their power structure and social institutions by means of an in-depth consideration of the other's diversity, its theoretical and practical implications for one's own set of beliefs and life style.

Both power and truth can undermine power. When power undermines power it is unreasonable to expect that it will be in itself responsive to any normative demand. What will follow in this case is the repetition of the same restrictive power structure, though power relations and representations may and will change. When power is undermined by truth, power structures grow in their complexity as they expand the ties of solidarity and the practical possibilities for self-relation. When power undermines power social inclusion results in homogenization and individual and social action, though maybe more diverse, grow in contradiction and self-destructiveness. When power undermines power, social structures remain at the service of (victorious) power and a society likewise established is no better or fairer than the previous one.

When respect to social diversity is simply justified in terms of group's right to self-determination, respect is being demanded from and to the other's power. Because power is in itself only respectable in its strength, an apparently more tolerant society is only the more cautious or fearful of the other's power. The discourse of self-determination departs from the assertion of value, without asking about those unavoidable conditions that make possible such assertion. On the other hand, when respect to the diversity of human societies is understood and justified in terms of the redeemable truth claims that this diversity implies, what is being respected is the uniqueness of each person and collectivity and what is fostered is freedom as increased self-understanding. What communities have to say is valuable in the first place because it represents an irreplaceable contribution to the validation and understanding of everyone's claims. Commitment with understanding, in its turn, demands and enforces power structures that are at the service of mutual understanding.

Approximations to any universalizable reality are compromised when the diversity of human perspectives and values are *a priori* asserted *or* denied. Respect to different cultures and life styles, even though an apparently self-sufficient demand and just cause, should be normatively grounded. The question "why should people's diverse world views and ways of life, their truth claims and power representations, be respected" is of fundamental significance for re-defining power structures and determining paths of action. Both those who favor and those who attack development answer this question in a very similar way, with most oppressive results for the peoples of the world, both in Western and non-Western, modern and traditional societies.

By denying people the possibility of redeeming their claims, either because there is no truth or because science is the only discourse whose claims have been authorized as redeemable, the development debate justifies mutual respect on the discourse of "rights". Both sides in the debate are thus validating and actualizing one and the same aspect of reality. This shared truth, a legacy of Enlightenment, is so powerful indeed that it still has not been replaced in the mind of social theorists and the way they conceive human action and interactions, in spite of all criticism that Modernity and Enlightenment have received almost since their inception.

Development and antidevelopment discourses, building on this modern achievement, hope that by destroying the possibility of agreement on higher realities, the grounds for practical domination will also be undermined. But although this reasoning may free people from the oppression of particular elites – either internal, such as local authority and traditional hierarchies or external ones, such as submission to the demands of the global market and international players – it frees them to either repeat traditionally established patterns of action or to pursue ever new trends of consumption, that is, to pursue nothing substantially meaningful. The threat of others is in this case replaced by a self imposed destruction.

I have already explained the internal contradictions of this reasoning and why the way it justifies mutual respect to human diversity is self-defeating. I have also started a discussion on why conceiving human condition from another perspective would be more consistent with the goal of mutual respect. I will next continue to reflect on this possibility as I explain mutual respect in tandem with self-understanding. In general terms, it can be said that if equality and freedom lie in everyone's capacity to understand and fulfill particular purposes; and if understanding is a function of validation, then the possibility of knowing the truth is not oppressive, it cannot determine the absolute knowledge of some and the ignorance of others, endow the first with power while depriving the second.

The Condition of Mutual Respect

To build mutual respect on the grounds of individual right is to expect survival to stand as a self-referential goal. Although self-preservation or survival is in human beings a constitutive aspect of the drive towards self-understanding, this observation – contrary to how the social and human studies literature has interpreted it – implies that the drive for self-understanding is the condition of possibility of survival and not the other way around. While without survival there is no self-understanding, the one who understands may well decide to give up his life for the understanding he has achieved. In the absence of understanding and meaning, however, survival is purposeless and constantly under threat.

We know almost instinctively that survival is not a self-referential goal for human beings. It is enough to ask why saving another person's life is a normal expectation for everyone but not saving the life of a cow or a tree. Regardless of the particular ways in which people answer this question, one can only be (must be) responsive to those appeals that he understands. If we all understood the appeals of cows and trees, the decision to still go ahead and kill them would have necessarily to be accountable to this personal understanding and the reasons we would have and give to kill them would be fundamentally different from the ones we had before such understanding. It is the possibility of understanding the demand of the other that places a responsibility on us and the better these appeals are understood the more comprehensive the response will be.

If we take one step further in our reasoning, we come to the realization that it is not simply the understanding of the other's demand that bind people together in a relation of responsibility. The condition of understanding itself is its validation in terms of its correspondence to the objective world of facts, the intersubjective world of social norms and one's own subjective inner experiences.[3] If our initial understanding is proven false and the cry unworthy of help, either according to our group's norms and expectations, to our personal trajectory of life or simply because the other was not actually crying or was faking it, our response will be different from what our first understanding, would have determined. Our response to a cry for help is continuously re-validated as we act and it is this validation of one's response which allows for a particular action. Relations of mutual respect or oppression are a function of how validation is carried out, that is, whether it includes the one we are responding to or whether it gradually excludes him.

---

3   See Habermas (1990a) for a comprehensive explanation of these three claims of validity that are simultaneously raised in human communication and which confer it intelligibility.

The first requirement for demanding and reasonably expecting mutual respect is the assumption that the subject understands the other's request, which simultaneously implies the capacity to validate one's own understanding and response with the other. The decision to respect people's diversity lies in the subject awareness of the requirements of validation and its implications for self-relation. As the subject grows in the awareness of the contingent incoherencies of his action in relation to the non-contingent structure of this action – which requires continuous re-validation in order to be understandable – he can choose to validate his action with the other, keeping in this way the integrity of his self-relation.

Mutual respect represents the possibility of redeeming pre-established objective knowledge, social norms and personal intentions. It is a particular form of response that is in agreement with what response to the other in general represents: the inclusion of the other in the validation of previous knowledge. Mutual respect is the readiness to re-evaluate what we are doing in light of the claims that the other raises, reassessing in this way our own place in the order of things.

When this relation between understanding and mutual respect, along with its practical implications for the self-relation of individuals and communities, is excluded from the defense of rights, oppression takes place, either overtly or in a concealed manner. An oppressive relation is one that fosters a fragmented self-relation and does not allow for a coherent self-understanding – regardless of whether survival is immediately under threat or not. When one party, in his response to another, does not include the other in the validation of the truth, correctness and truthfulness of his understanding of the other's claims, self-understanding is impaired for all parties and oppression takes place. Oppression is a self-imposed limitation on understanding that results from responding to the other *as if* the other's question (and response) had no effect in one's own understanding. It is a contradictory action that results from an impaired perception of the ties that *already* brought the sides together in the relation of oppression. Oppression limits the one who excludes to the struggle for survival and denies him the most fundamental right: the right to know his self.

Oppression is reproducing the same established interpretations of the truth, the good and the truthful and acting thus without knowledge of cause other than guaranteeing survival, as if social recognition is the overarching possibility for social interaction. As I discussed earlier, when social recognition is thus perceived, pre-validated social symbols take over freedom and determine the facts, the norms and the intentions that are to be materialized in society. This kind of oppressive recognition, which I defined as ethical recognition, is what a self-referential demand for mutual respect to the other's right can promote.

When we do not inquiry into the value of our unique choices and symbols to the uniqueness of others, these choices begin to oppress us. We *reproduce* them and what would have been original creations out of fear of losing our capacity to judge and discern between true and false, good and bad, truthful and dishonest. The fear is to put one's capacity of understanding and judgment at the mercy of another and lose, in this process, one's sense of integrity. Oppression is bred by the fear of having the validity of one's symbols questioned, their value diminished or lost, and together with it the confidence that the self is capable of understanding and realization.

The fear to lose, with the inclusion of the other, what has been validated and held valuable, perhaps throughout generations, is also the fear of losing those references according to which the self has learned about his capacities and built an integrated trajectory. The possibility of losing one's sense of self or integrity is at the core of the human struggle for self-preservation. Paradoxically, this struggle leads to oppressive relations and to the disintegration of the self. We exclude the other, even when *already* responding to him, because having a sense of self is an overarching value and because the other so essentially affects this sense. The perception of the other's power explains why even those who represent no threat to another's physical survival still fall victim of oppression, exploitation and downgrading treatment. In order to protect our well-established understanding and sense of self we may shun away from the other, avoiding altogether the risks *and* possibilities of this affect. Afraid that we may not get what we want, we give up the possibility of getting it at all. Oppression is thus established.

The development debate defines oppression as a unilateral and other-directed relation, as it understands power as a possession, either individual or collective. They claim, therefore, that oppression is the disempowerment of some and that the power of each has to be restituted, as every individual or collectivity has the right to exercise his power without interference and without interfering in the power of others. Nonetheless, when power is understood in these terms, ultimately at the service of self-preservation, it cannot overcome oppression and liberate people. Any particular use of power will oppress and this oppression – though in some exceptional cases less oppressive to the so called oppressed – will unavoidably oppress the oppressor.

Power can only enhance community and personal lives when understood as an expression of the drive towards self-understanding. No matter how much developmentists struggle to spread Western symbols around the world with the sincere or strategic desire to liberate people from the constraints of nature and its community's oppressive traditions; no matter how much they desire to see communities respecting its members' rights and freedom to decide about their own future; and no matter how antidevelopmentists struggle against the homogenization of cultures, the submission of local forms of life to the imperatives of impersonal systems; how they try to restore communities' power to decide about their own present and future; oppression will still set in, growing and reproducing itself in ever new power relations and representations. And moreover, it won't oppress some and not others, it will oppress *everyone*, from modern Western to traditional non-Western societies and local communities.

If power is not to oppress the beholder it should be approached as the all-inclusive power of human interactions to advance self-understanding. Looking at the current seemingly uneven distribution of the power to survive, the argument that power cannot be monopolized nor redistributed, seem at best purposeless.

However, if monopoly is a possibility then the next logical question one should answer is: what would take those with more power to stop using it in their own advantage, that is, as a means to accumulate more power? In other words, what could alter such trend in human relations, even though the actors in power may and are continuously changing?

As we have seen, antidevelopmentists have (unsuccessfully) tried to answer this question through an effort to discursively undermine what seems to be the foundation of development power: its pretension to embody and be the spokesman of truth. As a result, they have re-asserted the truth of survival and re-placed communities' rich potentialities and diverse expressions at the service of mere self-preservation.

If the life style of a community is not to be universally judged and evaluated and has to be accepted for its own sake – or even if it is to be criticized only by those who partake in it – the purpose of social order is eventually reduced to self-preservation. Agreement on other purposes is perceived as unattainable and, as a result, those societies more fearful of death will accumulate more power in the struggle for self-preservation. If the right of the community should be respected only for purposes of self-preservation, accumulation of power cannot be, either discursively or practically, restrained. If, on the other hand, communities are environments that foster self-understanding, power can be understood (and expressed) in a different manner.

Power and the Search for Self-understanding

The development debate can at best succeed in altering the *composition* of power relations but not its *structure*, as it overlooks the fact that the right of individuals to self-assertion or the right of communities to self-determination is purposeless if one cannot *continuously* validate the meaning of his choices. Regardless of the particular and diverse ways in which people assert their capacities, self-assertion and self-determination are dirempted self-understanding. As such, although they give the impression of being able to at least temporarily protect established truths, they do not fulfill the purpose towards which such protection was impelled, they do not validate understanding.

Understanding one's choices, the condition of self-assertion, means knowing that one is able to perform *valid* actions, that is, not random, purposeless movements. Self-assertion, even as dirempted reality, presupposes the assent of the other, without which value could not be determined and every choice would be nothing but an accidental event. Concomitantly, self-assertion must deal with the ever present possibility of "assent withdrawal". The other may at any moment, as an individual or as a group, not validate my actions. For this reason self-assertion, as a set of external and internal mechanisms to cope with the possibility of withdrawal and to reduce the risk of its actualization, seems to prevail in human relations, rather than self-understanding.

Because the condition of possibility of validation, nonetheless, is a symmetric relation between free and creative agents, the subject's effort to understand and realize his capacities, excluding from this process the "withdrawal" power of the other, and likewise his original response, brings validation down to pre-validation and limits the possibility of understanding to that "which the subject already new". Self-assertion is self-defeating because it tries to *preserve* the non-conservable validity of understanding, the meaning of action and the value of the subject, by pre-determining, at the level of principle, the actors who can question the validity of action and the doubts that can be raised against action. The self-assertive subject, proud of his gain, that is, satisfied with the impossibility of further losses, as he seeks to avoid the unpredictable word of the other, brings to mind the picture of a lover who takes away his beloved's life to keep her forever by.

The question about the value of one's capacities and the meaning of one's actions is constitutive of life in any society, whether it pursues the preservation of physical life and fosters those capacities and institutions that allow for this preservation or whether it values more transcendental and non-material ends. At a most basic level of awareness one wonders whether what he does corresponds to what his society validates and values.[4] At another stage of consciousness, or maybe at a more advanced stage of moral development and rationality, as some would argue,[5] the question becomes how valid are socially validated objective reality, norms and intentions. The question for the subject – particularly or maybe only in modern times – is whether there is anything truer, better and more truthful and thus fairer than the established social choices.

The drive that fosters exclusionist self-assertion and the struggle for the accumulation of power, on the one hand, or inclusion and cooperation, on the other, is the drive towards understanding. We are, in other words, compelled to know that what we believe in, what we do and want to pursue corresponds to reality, that is, that we are not being deceived in our judgment of what is true, what is good and what is truthful. It could be argued that people do not carry their lives in a state of constant doubt and that the basis for intentional action is actual trust in the validity of judgment. It is important to clarify, for this reason, that the fact that the requirements of validity rend it vulnerable and make it an uncertain endeavor, does not imply that the person, in reflection, will doubt his judgment – a state, moreover, closer to the pathological and that would certainly paralyze action. What the understanding of these requirements does imply is that the person will not exclude, on the basis of any other commitment, another one who doubts and expects a response from him.

Self-assertion or self-determination, the object of the development debate, is not impelled by power but by the search for truth. The assertion of one's capacity involves doing what is right and knowledge of what is right. As long as we ignore

---

4   Kohlberg's (1981) theory of moral development sets forth the structure for this explanation.

5   See, for instance, Kohlberg (1981), Habermas (1990a) and Edgerton (1992).

the conditions that make self-assertion possible, however, our struggle seems reduced to self-preservation and our will only to power, a power that, moreover, cannot be shared. In order to preserve the validity of understanding and the actions that result thereof, we may have to destroy or weaken potential threats as we try to remove their power. But the pursuit of power through the disempowerment of the other happens only when one party possesses what is valuable for another, that is, what one understands to be valuable. And this is either a literal possession or a negative threat to one's values. No one tries to dispossess another of something that he just happens to have.

The implication of this apparently self-evident account is that the will to power is impelled by the will to truth and not the other way around. Therefore, although power relations may change, as the contingent result of the relative strength of the actors that are struggling to preserve a particular self-understanding, it is not an increase or accumulation of power what can change the structure of power relations in a particular society. Only when the *way* people validate truth changes, is power undermined. Any struggle for self-preservation, either explained in terms of self-assertion or self-determination, is the irony of a war for truth carried on in the battlefields of power.

The power that restitutes self-preservation to its original place cannot be held by some against others, cannot be taken away and cannot be accumulated. It is a power that can only exist within all-inclusive relationships. If to *preserve* that which is valuable we may need to destroy the other, in order to *know* what is valuable we always need the other. As the value and desirability of a reality cannot be determined in isolation, the other is a *sine qua non* condition for determining what is valuable.

The answer to the question of what would stop those more successful in self-preservation, or more powerful, by traditional accounts, to use their power against others and towards the further accumulation of power, is awareness of the condition of possibility of self-preservation. It may be argued that although validation is a collective process it does not require, however, universal inclusion and that local communities would be the best environment for establishing symmetrical relations and determining what the truth, good and beautiful are. This argument, nonetheless, for the reasons already exposed, would leave the question unanswered and not challenge the prevailing power structures.

To the argument that local communities are the practical setting for determining value and meaning it should be added that, normatively speaking and if these local relations are to validate reality, they cannot deny answering to *any* demand for validation, whether from within or outside the community. Failure to do so is to compromise the process of validation and engage in self-denial, that is, to pretend that that which (still) has not been validated is valid. When one is looking for truth, any exclusions imply deviating one's search.

Even when we adopt the easy attitude of "each to its own", we are impelled to know how real "our own" is. The argument that the structure of validation is universal does not imply that people are actively seeking at every moment to know what is *universally valid*. But since we are impelled to know that what we do even in our most private moments is the best for us, not being accountable to every other claim that speaks to ours is an impossible trial in self-deception: the raising to the status of truth that which is only too frail to stand exposure.

Power, in the normative context of universal inclusion, is not directed to the preservation of truth but to the increasing of understanding. It is, therefore, a power that cannot be with some and not with others. As people's perception of reality are irreplaceable in this process, there is no symbol or pre-validated understanding which would endow a particular group or individual with more power, turning them into a threat against another. Each reality that is re-validated clarifies the incompleteness of understanding and the possibility of further understanding.

This re-conceptualization of power maintains from its traditional definition the intentionality of action. But since this intentionality is necessarily directed to a meaningful end, power as *meaningful* action cannot be hindered by or hinder somebody else's *meaningful* actions. Because meaning cannot be preserved, actions will certainly change in interaction as understanding changes, that is, as new truths are validated. This change, however, does not imply a reduction or limitation on one's power.

To the extent that social symbols and values, material and non-material productions, are the expression of each people's unique way of validating the world, to dominate and to destroy or devalue them as lesser expressions of truth is to weaken one's own power of understanding and meaningful action. If a society that has more physical power to survive and to perpetuate its symbols uses this power as a means to reduce the survival power of another, power can only attend to the fear of death, unable to release the capacities of the "powerful" and to foster meaningful production and impairing indeed the self-understanding of all the affected.

If, on the other hand, this material advantage is open to universal questioning and ready to justify the actions of the beholder, it will become the unique contribution of a society to the understanding of all. In this case, superior techniques and material advantages would not turn society into oppressive but into the fosterer of collective self-understanding. This society can contribute with the expression of other dimensions of people's potentialities, to the extent that its unique characteristics ask for the revalidation of other people's achievements and must, in its turn, be validated by them.

While ancient and post-axial philosophers thought that only a fateful future would bring power and truth together because truth was an independent reality, standing beyond and above human life and not necessarily powerful, the Enlightenment asserted the normative as well as the contingent unity of truth and power. For the moderns, anyone can know the truth, embedded as it is in daily life and ordinary human endeavors. Thus conceived, truth does not threaten power but actually supports it. Although the critics of modernity invert this logic, they also would agree that power and truth do coincide, as power appropriates or invents those truth claims necessary for its own perpetuation.

Power is indeed founded on truth claims but, contrary to prevailing understanding, the structure of these claims does not exclude nor *a priori* invalidates other claims. It does raise the *pretension* of universal validity but, precisely for this reason, claims demand to be universally validated in the contingent interaction between peoples and societies. To act otherwise, that is, to exclude, oppress and dominate because one's understanding of reality validates and authorizes such actions, is to act in a self-defeating manner. It not only sets limits to the possibility of validation and thus understanding but it also irremediably impairs power. When the possibility of universal validation is denied, power becomes self-destructive. Without its normative guide, it becomes an arbitrary force, destroying not only the other but also eventually the beholder themself.

Social alternatives that ignore the condition of power cannot foster a better or fairer society. The demand for universal respect to the diversity of life styles and cultures fosters in this case a corrupt or desvirtuated power structure. When a person or a group do not or cannot engage in the universal validation of their choices, everyone's *search* for the truth is sacrificed for the preservation of a self that seeks in the defeating and betraying power of exclusion a refuge against death. Because the truth can only be validated in all-inclusive relationships, awareness of human interdependency in the search for truth is what would allow reorienting the dirempted struggle for survival towards an inclusive search for self-understanding.

Power as a means to protect and perpetuate social symbols is an effort to actualize human unity through misguided efforts. It tries to achieve its goal through a shortcut: by avoiding the risks and possible losses that relations of recognition pose to one's value, that is, by securing recognition only through power. Recognition thus granted is, however, of no value to the receiver. Simultaneously, the misuse of power makes manifest the social nature of that which is being pursued, no matter how much power tries to detach the aimed object from its original condition – by setting imaginary boundaries and creating a self-sufficient collectivity to purportedly replace the irreplaceability of the other.

Truth and power, differently than how ancients saw it and contrary to the diremption that modernity set in motion, are inseparable. Understanding is unique for each person and the more everyone participates in validating the truth of objective facts, the righteousness of social norms, and the truthfulness of intentions, the more peoples' diverse capacities are fulfilled. Knowledge of truth is not a privilege of some, because knowledge changes as participation expands and increases. Universal participation may be a practical impossibility, though easier to conceive in this time and age. But understanding the purpose and requirements of such participation is fundamental if we are to question the validity of established knowledge and correct the diremptions of our daily practice.

Although power cannot be detached from the requirements of truth, it can be misused as it tries to preserve particular truths. On the other hand, power can respect such requirements and, as such, promote personal and community development. We can say that power is in this case no longer only an expression of truth, but that it actively fosters knowledge of truth. Our next question, therefore, should be: What would be the practical expression of the all-inclusive relation that the unity of truth and power calls for? Or yet, how do we have to interact in order to promote a development that is committed with the search for truth? From the perspective of human unity, development is an activity that brings together power and truth through the process of dialogue.

PART III
Redefining Development

Introduction to Part III

The real community of man, in the midst of all the self-contradictory simulacra of community, is the community of those who seek the truth, of the potential knowers, that is, in principle, of all men to the extent they desire to know. ... Their common concern for the good linked them; their disagreement about it proved they needed one another to understand it. This is ... the only real friendship, the only real common good. It is here that the contact people so desperately seek is to be found. The other kinds of relatedness are only imperfect reflections of this one trying to be self-subsisting, gaining their only justification from their ultimate relation to this one. (Bloom 1987: 381)

The development debate, standing for or against development theory and practice, builds on different arguments and arrives at the same conclusions. Whether emphatically stating the problems of poverty and the importance of individual rights and self-assertion and claiming the universal status of this problem and its corresponding solution; or whether criticizing these truth claims and, as a matter of fact, the possibility of any other truth, in the name of community's right to self-determination, developmentists and antidevelopmentists are validating one and the same reality. To define the requirement of freedom in terms of non-interference is to equate people's struggle with the preservation of their physical and symbolic self, defeating thus the purpose of freedom, either as an individual or collective exercise.

Nonetheless, as long as one talks of how human beings *should* be treating each other – as the parties in the development debate do – rather than simply describe the state of their interaction, the impossibility of referring to human beings as any other phenomenon in the world is, from within the structure of one's own discourse, being revealed. In referring to an *ought* we expect a level of response and understanding that is shared exclusively among human beings. We assume a level of unity among interlocutors, factual or potential ones, that allows us to denounce our actions and demand changes from each other. Because of this unity, we can demand that communities respect individual freedom or that Western societies do not interfere with the way of life of other communities. The underlying assumption behind such requests is that we share common qualities that make the content and the intention of our claim understandable.

The development debate suffers in this way from a main inconsistency: the content of its demands does not address the unavoidable structure of such demands. The inconsistency rests in asking *humans* to be accountable for a non-human behavior. Hence, even in the case that such demands were by themselves attainable – what would mean that we would be able to momentarily put our human dimension on hold – they could only be heard and answered by human beings and not by any other living creature, whose capacities are oriented towards self-preservation alone.

There are, however, discursive and practical alternatives that are coherent with the human condition, with those traits that human beings share exclusively with one another and that determine their interdependency at the human level. In this sense development is possible. It refers to an alternative that realizes and respects human unity. Away from such realization any proposal would result in an effort to prolong human life and for this purpose people do not need social scientists. People's natural instincts, and natural science at best, suffice. But at the moment social or natural scientists start explaining *why* peoples' lives should be protected, even if for *its own sake* – as it happens with the discourse of modern rights, with the self-justifying end of modern science and with the defense of cultural diversity – they are appealing to a value beyond life itself and evoking more than people's survival instincts.

To argue for development is to re-direct the *human* struggle for survival or the need for social recognition to its implied end. We develop to the extent that we engage in the universal validation of understanding, that is, in the expansion of self-understanding or, still, to the extent that we express our unique and socially relevant capacities at the service of everyone else's development. Any society that does not promote the self-understanding of its members cannot claim to be developed. It is a society that is changing, hardly surviving but not developing. Moreover, because of our condition of unity, development is a collective trait. It can only be achieved within the community of peoples and nations. To the degree a person or a community develops he is determining everyone else's development. And to the extent that the other is excluded from the development process, one's very own development is impaired. Differently from what development discourse would argue, development – and not survival alone – is impossible if it is not built on local and global relations of universal inclusion.

To talk in terms of developed and underdeveloped or developing countries is to set meaningless standards for human relations and for social change. As long as development is approached as a fragmented possibility, it ignores human unity and cannot point to anything but the temporary success of a society in self-preservation. As it stands now "developed" or First World countries are those who fear death the most, are most enslaved to their social symbols and have come up with the most elaborated mechanisms – science and technology – to preserve their life and symbols. In a globalized world, where human unity has not only to be recognized but also actualized in every community, we cannot say that some could or developing alone. What we have is an underdeveloped world that necessitates development.

Development becomes possible today to an extent that could not be achieved before the modern encounter of cultures and peoples. For the first time it is possible for the peoples of the world not only to *state* their unity – as some thinkers and philosophers have been doing for thousands of years[1] – but also to *respect* such condition through relations that are actually answerable to everyone's demand. Paradoxically, the likelihood of failing to develop is greater in a modern globalized world than ever before. Pre-modern and pre-globalized societies, although carrying its relations within the imperatives of human unity, did not have to face the challenge of having to include in their practical relations different cultures and communities and the consequences of failing at such an all-inclusive extent.

Although the possibility of development has always been more limited than it is today, as every human being could not partake in the process of validating the truth, pre-modern societies, likewise, could not exclude as much. Respect to human unity or equal respect to people's diversity becomes only gradually challenging as a greater diversity must be included in one's relations and according to increasingly more demanding standards of equality and social inclusion. The likelihood of exclusion under such circumstances, or at least identifying and denouncing its many expressions, becomes understandably higher. These circumstances brought up by globalization and the new challenges posed to the respect of human unity, is what makes for the particularity of human development in this day and time.

Development, due to the condition of human unity, could never be partial, the achievement of some and not of others. People and communities could and have been developing, however, within the limits that the absence of the other has allowed for. They did it without what the uniqueness of the other had to contribute to their own self-understanding. The implications of this absence for the process of self-understanding are different, however, than the active choice to exclude the other. Once "discovery" happens, the other must be heard and answered. If communities were developing within the limits of given possibilities, this "discovery" subsumes development to the new relation that is established, which can either be of inclusion or active exclusion. Ignoring each other, or ignoring human interdependence, does not entail a limited development alone, that is, the unaltered permanence of previous achievements. It implies engaging in a cycle of self-oppression and self-alienation, where development is deviated into the preservation of what has turned now into meaningless symbols.

The general structure of this argument can be better understood with an illustration taken from human physical development. The persistence of child like patterns of behavior in a fully grown adult determines a pathological condition, no matter how relevant earlier acquired skills were to the further development of the individual. The requirements of development at a later stage, moreover, are not those of an earlier stage. An adult that insists on being nursed, for instance, is not only hampering his future development, but also threatening the overall health which he has acquired throughout his life. In other words, the gains of the past are threatened by the unattended demands of the present.

---

1   See Heater (1996) for a recount of the history of world citizenship, for instance, in Western thought.

Although in the context of our discussion a "developing society" is not oriented to a pre-determined end, historically speaking societies have "grown" in integration following the trend of diversification and complexification. As social relations expand and become more inclusive, the requirements for society's continuing development also change. But diversification and complexification, while determining a new stage in society's life and themselves the result of previous developments, are not yet the measure or sufficient condition for development.[2] These circumstances bring forth the requirement to include the other in a *particular way* – a way of inclusion that has not and could not be before. Similarly, at the moment a society, following historical trends, "grows" or expands its relations, the choice of exclusion, in the name of old and accepted patterns of behavior, poses a novel and fatal threat to all previous social gains.

To argue that communities were thriving well in isolation before the modern colonization and expansions and that they, for this reason, can still live independently from one other or to claim, on the other hand, that as a consequence of the global economy some communities have been and can be excluded or marginalized, is to literally maintain *all* the peoples of the world in a pathological state of retardation. It is to ask communities and people to keep behaving and interacting according to standards that do not respond to the requirements determined by the new levels of integration they undertook. It is to expect that the once self-sufficient society that was able to grow and develop without others will still be able do it in an age of globalization and intense cross-cultural migrations. Societies that try this pattern of action are irremediably impairing their own continued development and eventually their integrity.

Human development requires abidance to the demands of human interdependency, which are made evident through gradual social change. It is important to understand that the binding nature of human interdependency is not similar to the one brought in by the trends of globalization. Although globalization does reveal the condition of human unity, the demands that it imposes are only the ones made evident and required by this condition. The contingent interdependency that the development discourse identifies, and according to which it wants to justify its global and all-inclusive project, does not bind people to irreversible demands nor can it determine the measure of human development.

Because development theory and practice recognize in the current trends of social change the possibility of development, it can only address and foster the struggle for self-preservation. Whether referring to economic, environmental or security needs and talking about a "common future", "environmental planning" or "peacekeeping strategies", the underlying theme is always an evolving world that has grown too interconnected in the fulfillment of its survival needs for each part to survive on its own. Although current social changes reveal the interdependency

---

2   Although the principles for a theory of social justice have been laid out in terms of increased individuation and social inclusion – Honneth (1992) – I question how sufficient these principles are for delineating normative criteria for a theory of social critique.

of all living creatures and, consequently, make the argument that everyone's and every living creature's survival is indeed purposeful, to reduce *human* interdependency to this contingent level is misleading and defeats the purpose of survival itself.

Any kind of human relation, including the one that seeks the survival of the species, is always submitted to a relation that human beings establish first with one another as humans or beings capable of mutual understanding. This means that, as I have explained it earlier, though relations do not require actual universal participation in the particular function and purpose that they serve, these relations are only possible because they imply a non-contingent level of interaction where *everyone's* claims are irreplaceable. The demand for universal respect to people's and nature's rights should be built on this basis and not because of a survival that is threatened by everyone and everything in the globalized world that has been created.

When development claims a global and all-inclusive scope for its project in the name of a "common future", its goal obviously is not simply to promote security and survival but to do it so that other purposes can be fulfilled. Nonetheless, a development process that is aware of the human condition of unity would justify its actions the other way around. The achievement of more transcendental purposes cannot be sought through the immediate concern with the preservation of peoples' life. It is through our effort to achieve higher purposes that our life *may* also be preserved. The search for these purposes may put survival at risk because, as we have too many times witnessed, any sacrifice is acceptable for the one who achieves meaning – unfortunately not only self but also other's sacrifice – and, likewise, life is not worth for the one who sees no meaning.

The goal of development project to preserve people's life or to promote global survival in order to guarantee the conditions for other and higher forms of realization is, therefore, a misconception of the human condition and its success a practical impossibility. Such misconception and impossibility are evidenced in the substantial efforts of modern science and technology to face and alleviate the paradoxically destructive side-effects of promoting security and well-being. Even in the apparently successful cases where medical science, for instance, has increased people's life span, an achievement that the defenders of modernity and development always hold as a checkmate against its critics,[3] it is highly contestable what the value of such gain would represent for a society that does not foster meaningful relations. It is sadly telling that so many species live significantly longer under captivity and that yet no one would consider captivity a victory gained for the wild life.

The goal of any development project should be the promotion of those institutions and relations that respect human unity and allow for its fulfillment. In other words, to actively try to develop people's and communities' capacities within relations that abide to the requirements of human interdependency. Survival would

---

3 See, for instance, Edgerton (1992).

be the result of communities' release of their unique capacities. Different modes of survival would be the creative expression of each community's search for self-understanding. Development proposals could be in this case originated in any community and would address, directly or indirectly, all others. They would never be centralized, directed from one group, typically those who have accumulated more instruments of survival, to another – those who have accumulated less, most likely because their fear of death has not been as much.

It is difficult to imagine within the present dominant framework of development theory and practice that the people of Brazil, Ethiopia or Afghanistan should be proposing alternatives for the development of people in the United States, Germany and England. But this is precisely the only way development would be feasible. Because the accumulation of particular symbols cannot tell anything about the level of human development – just about their possible capacities, which in any case would have to be re-validated – and because development as self-understanding requires an active contribution to the other, suggestions and projects have to originate in every community and be addressed potentially to all others.

Development as the release of people's capacities and qualities can only be promoted today through an all-inclusive relation that listens to what each person and community has to say to the others. This means that society seriously hampers the understanding and expression of its member's capacities and those of other communities if it cannot or does not accept to revalidate its own symbols and potential achievements with every other society.

Here again the all-inclusive nature of human development is different from the all-inclusiveness that modern development project seeks to promote. The latter departs from a mistaken assumption of the human condition and is carried out in a unilateral way, where some are the knower, the planners and the givers of development to others. This other is the simple receiver of development benefits. Even when he is seen as a crucial participant in this process and his engagement actively sought by well intended development agents who are trailing the path of "grassroots" development, his role is reduced to *informing* the development planner of his needs, community's limits and strengths, as if these were readily accessible and a possible piece of information.[4] The receiver of development brings to mind in this case the image of a patient undergoing surgery who is kept partially awake in order to "guide" the doctor. To call the patient, no matter how crucial his role is to the final outcome of the procedure, a "participant" is at best an ironic depiction of the patient/doctor relationship.

Modern development project is all-inclusive because it claims that no people or society should be left out from the benefits of modern knowledge and technology. Everyone should be acquainted with the Western way of life and hold its symbols. No matter what noble purposes and how well intended the agents of this type of development are, they would, in the most successful but unlikely case, promote

---

4   This is the case even with well-intended development projects and proposals. See, for example, Yunus (2007) and Singer (2009).

people's equal survival. They would create a global society based on the same modes of survival (Western science and technology) and, as a society primordially committed with survival, it would gradually become homogenized in all other aspects of life. This homogenized global society would be always at the brink of self-destruction, its survival without purpose and as such constantly threatened.

The development that respects human unity is all-inclusive not in its end results, which determines homogenization, but in its beginning. In a globalized world, development happens to the extent that every community expresses those capacities that can be validated by everyone else as fostering the expression of everyone's capacities. Development is not the simple assertion of a well-established and socially valued capacity, without regards for what it says to other people and how this other validates it. Besides, if one's actions are not re-validated, they can hardly be considered the expression of one's unique potentialities. Even if, for instance, science and technology can be agreed to represent Western's unique way of surviving, this recognition cannot be *a priori* granted. It will have to be validated with the peoples of the world and, in this process, re-appropriated by Western societies themselves. Only within this continuous validation can these symbols be an expression of Western's unique capacity and cease to be both a trivial reproduction of established patterns of recognition and a tool of oppression.

The development of human capacities has no givers and beneficiaries, knower and ignorant, developed and underdeveloped sides. It is a collective and global effort of people who come together not to survive but to validate and thus understand the meaning and the unique value of the ways in which each is surviving.

The development of people's capacities poses a next practical question. As I have reiterated, the development of people's capacities or self-understanding and realization can only be a collective process as it depends on the relations of recognition in which people participate. At this stage of the argument, our next question should be: by what means can we develop, rather than simply *try* to survive collectively? What kind of practical relation is all-inclusive in its structure and not only in its goal? Or still, what power can get us closer to our true self, that is, what kind of action brings the power and the truth of the human condition together? The answer to these questions is the same: dialogue. In order for truth to release its power it has to be assessed in a dialogical manner. And it is the understanding of the meaning and implications of this procedure for human development, or for individual and community freedom, what is missing and has to be retrieved in the development debate and in both side's practical projects and proposals.

Dialogue is the power that represents the truth of human unity in its fullest sense or the practical action that reflects awareness of this human condition. Whenever people, at whatever level of interaction, decide to engage in dialogue – and not simply in some kind of communication – its structure is inevitably respecting the unity of human beings and promoting collective self-understanding. Regrettably for the advancement of social critique, neither development nor antidevelopment discourse have proposed global dialogue as the way for respecting and fostering personal and community's diverse capacities.

In the absence of dialogue, power is inevitably at the service of survival, uphold by everyone's fear of death and the apparent possession of some and the desire of others. Dialogue, on the other hand, is the power that everyone has while recognizing his or her fundamental unity with everyone else. Dialogue is the expression of this unity and the fulfillment of its purpose, that is, the realization of people's diversity. In what follows I will examine how dialogue expresses the reality of human unity and advances understanding. I will then continue the discussion I began here on human development with a characterization of the type of community that is required as dialogue is undertaken within and between societies.

Chapter 6
The Truth and Power of Dialogue

Dialogue is the process of giving and demanding reasons for the sole purpose of reaching understanding. It is a process that is rarely found in its pure form in human relations but which, at the same time, is the normative condition of the practical possibility of any human communication, no matter how diverted and corrupt in its purposes. Human beings can communicate because of the most basic assumption that mutual understanding is possible. Even in deceitful communication the interlocutor hopes to be understood in what he is literally saying in order not to be understood in what he keeps from saying.[1]

Dialogue, furthermore, is a universal process. It accepts and answers every demand for justification. Because its sole commitment is with reaching the best possible understanding at a given moment, anyone who doubts the validity of what is being said could in principle demand that the claims being raised in dialogue be validated. Any other commitment or alliances become partial and subordinated to the goal of mutual understanding and the *a priori* exclusion of any claim is thus self-defeating. Reasons should be given and demanded until all the interlocutors or participants in dialogue accept that truth claims have been redeemed for the time being.

Participants in dialogue may engage and will engage therein with their particular and personal interests. To the extent that they seek to validate these interests with every other potential interlocutor, that is, through dialogue, these interests will change until they become understandable and acceptable to all other participants. When this collective validation of an originally personal interest happens – or when one redeems the *social value* of his choice in terms of its correspondence with the objective reality, with the intersubjective world of norms and traditions and with the subjective intentions that constitutes his life-long biography – we can say that the person has gone through the re-appropriation of his interests and expresses unique capacities. This process happens within the limits and to the extent that society as a whole has reached a higher level of understanding and integration.

Dialogue allows participants a comprehensive assessment and validation of truth, that is, the understanding of the truth of objective statements, the fairness

---

1   See Habermas (1990a).

of social norms of coexistence and the righteousness of personal choice. This understanding, contrary to prevailing assumptions, has necessarily to be inclusive of all processes of knowledge, that is, inclusive of modern science, religious traditions, and autochthones knowledge. Differently from a conversation carried among insiders alone, dialogue is a process open to the questioning of everyone, including non-experts and alien cultures alike. Furthermore, the latter are not only allowed participating in the simultaneous validation of the claims raised in these three spheres but also with their own standards of validation. In dialogue these recently differentiated criteria of validation overlap and may even fuse and be transformed.

The modern differentiation of reality according to spheres of value, each with its own criteria of validation, is not necessarily a positive gain when looked at from the perspective of human unity and the requirements of an expanding understanding. The argument that social norms and traditions, for instance, do not have to be answerable to scientific advances and its new discoveries or that science utmost commitment is with the pursuit of its own self-sufficient and self-explanatory goals and is neutral in regards to ethical questions, poses several problems.[2] It represents a fallacy regarding the *structure* of normative and scientific claims because, in spite of differing criteria of validity, both spheres are in practice influenced and shaped by each other's goals and methods. It also represents a fallacy regarding their *status* as redeemed truths. The claim that the objective world, the subjective inner reality and the ethical norms and moral principles of a society constitute each independent spheres of reality is a truth claim only redeemable within particular contexts in modern societies and it does not find correspondence within the body of knowledge of any other contemporary non-modern society.[3] Consequently, this modern argument cannot promote an increased self-understanding as it delegitimizes *a priori* the participation of the majority of the world population in decisions that directly and indirectly affect their lives. This exclusion, in its turn, upholds a fragmented self, committed to contradictory claims as the *pretension of universal validity* that it implies does not carry a reconciliatory promise.

As individuals we have only an original intuition or perception of what is true. However, this personal understanding can grow in its correspondence with the truth when, in the process of dialogue, individual perceptions are gradually distanced from the basic drive to self-preservation and from the unquestioned reproduction of social conventions and symbols to get closer to a reality that expresses a universally validated and uniquely valuable self.

Contrary to how Enlightenment thinkers saw it and what the development debate sustains, agreement cannot be reached by lowering the human condition

---

2 Sandel (2010) addresses these problems in a comprehensive and eloquent manner.

3 For an analysis of some of the social implications of this modern differentiation of spheres of validity for the organization of non-modern contemporary societies see, for instance, Comaroff and Comaroff (2000) and Berman (2006). For an analysis of these implications for modern society itself see Bauman (1999).

to a struggle for individual and collective survival. This level of interaction gives rise to an antagonistic power structure where opposite groups try to suppress and destroy each other for the control and perpetuation of their means of survival. The search for meaning and self-understanding, as constitutive of the human condition, leads, on the other hand, to dialogue – a relation where everyone is allowed to question any truth claim and no established truth can be "unquestionable". And these will be questioned in their commitment with the preservation of a particular way of life.

In dialogue other reasons will be demanded besides the efficiency, coherency and truthfulness of one's personal and collective choices. Regardless of how a particular society or way of life is successful in dealing with natural events; how coherently it lives by what it preaches or succeeds in gradually closing the gap between its ideals and their institutionalization; and how transparently it stands by its will and intentions of self-preservation, these are not enough reasons for the redemption of one's choices in the context of international and multicultural relations. Societies that are technologically advanced and relatively just in the treatment of their own members still must have room in their actions and patterns of thought for completion and still must engage in convincing other societies that these actions call forth the uniqueness of the other's claims.

When we understand the value of giving reasons for what we do, for the way we live, for the decisions we make, we do not justify our action with the reasoning that "we do it this way because this is how we have always done it". If this is the only reason we have for our particular way of life there is indeed no purpose in enrolling in dialogue to solve our disagreements and conflicts. Those who enroll in dialogue are obviously not looking for the preservation of their choices. In dialogue each group's pattern of survival will be questioned and survival itself, not physical but symbolical, will *always* be under threat. But why would then someone enroll in such an apparently self-destructive action?

Willingness to submit our truths to dialogue streams from the awareness that the understanding of one's own original value requires a growing inclusion of the other, especially of those who contest and disagree with our choices. In this process one's mere existence can be transformed into the expression of a meaningful existence and this is the only promise embedded in dialogue. But since it is also the highest end one can hope for, it is worth the risk of a threatened self-relation.

Dialogue promotes an agreement on the value of each and everyone's capacities. At this level of agreement, different understandings do not contradict each other, giving raise to antagonist powers relations. By demanding reasons for each other's actions, the possibility is laid for understanding and validating one's choices according to its contributions to the realization of all. The universal validation of partial understandings reflects a temporary agreement *on what course or courses of action and patterns of thinking best reflect, at each moment, the diversity of capacities of those involved in actual dialogue.* And, once again, not that capacity or action which we assume as a society to be valuable, what would be the mere reproduction of established patterns of survival, but that capacity which everybody else can accept as valuable according also to their own (changing) criteria of validation.

It is only in dialogue that one is convinced of his or her *true* value, beyond what particular social systems, loyal to the imperatives of their own reproduction, may determine for the subject in terms of economic, religious or political value.[4] I call this "true" value because in dialogue one overcomes the self-deceitful nature of the monological struggle for the preservation of social roles. When the *universal other* is welcomed in questioning the value of this role, the subject is able to overcome his attachment to prevailing patterns of social recognition, which he might have been impelled to sustain as the only available means for self-understanding. To determine one's value in dialogue or through the active consent of the universal other is to validate social roles for their contributions to all and to redirect one's self-relation towards the honest pursuit of self-understanding or the understanding of true value.

Our true value consists in acting in such a way that every potential affected person can accept that those actions, at that moment, are taking him, in principle, closer to the understanding and expression of his own capacities and unique social value. Understanding the "truth" is not a static but a dynamic process which is always renewed as every person who does not find his or her particular understanding of the value of another represented in the prevailing agreement, renews dialogue and with it the opportunity to know the truth. When dialogue is called for, participants are given the opportunity to review their understanding of the truth under the light of a new singularity that asks them to justify previously unquestioned aspects of their social achievements.

Going back to the example of the human body, we can say that true value rests in those actions that allow every member of the body to contribute to the fulfillment of every other member's capacities. In this process disagreements on the best course of action have to be overcome and, similarly, mutual respect to the right of each to "do as they please" is not acceptable. Every member has to act as to promote the fulfillment of the others' capacities and will achieve self-realization within the regulatory limits of what every other member asks and allows for. On the other hand, no member is free to ask whatever he or she wants, independent from this same process which bides all the members to the singularity of each other. The true value of the eye and that of the hand, and of any other member of the body, lies in the fact that each fulfills its role as it tells and asks all others what it can be and do for them. For each member of the body there is a best way of action and this way is made evident as more members address the fulfillment of *all* others.

In human societies the only way to the fulfillment of peoples' real diversity, and not the arbitrary assertion of a meaningless difference, is dialogue. Dialogue is built on the consciousness of human unity and, at the same time, promotes it as

---

4   For an updated discussion on the colonization of the lifeworld by systems' imperatives see Hartmann and Honneth (2006).

it brings the understanding of the world, the power that it gives rise to and one's place within the world together.[5] Those who enroll in dialogue presuppose that understanding is only possible, that is, can only be validated as true and its power legitimized as good, in a relation between those who depend equally on each other for redeeming their claims. Human unity is for this reason fully recognized in the structure of dialogue and promoted in the dialogical act.

The Prerequisites of Dialogue

The most basic assumption of those who engage in dialogue is that there are *claims* about reality that are redeemable. Another assumption is that the *participant* himself has already some pre-understanding of this reality, which, nevertheless, is incomplete and can be advanced. One must believe that he knows something, something that the other can in principle understand and agree with, and at the same time not be absolutely convinced of this knowledge in order to participate in dialogue. If we did not accept that our claims are redeemable and that what we claim is also a fundamentally incomplete understanding, we could not engage in dialogue. This is the reason why those who believe that there is no redeemable truth; that everything is an arbitrary assertion of value, and ultimately of power; or still, believe in the possibility of an absolute knowledge, be it their own possession or somebody else's, can adopt any course of action but dialogue. Choices carried outside dialogue are, paradoxically, never one's own. They are the imposition of social structures and system's imperatives that perpetuate the cycle of a self-referential truth for another.

The third assumption of the participants in dialogue is that the *interlocutor* has an inalienable contribution to one's understanding, either with his consent or dissent. The other must, in principle, have a unique claim on our claims for dialogue to happen. This assumption implies the recognition of the value of the other's interpellation prior to any qualifications. Everyone who agrees or disagrees with our claims should be answered. Failure to do so and exclusion on the basis of any other commitment is a diremption of dialogue, which is solely committed with the goal of mutual understanding.

Human interdependence is the unavoidable condition of knowing, evidenced even in apparently non-dialogical methods of understanding, such as in meditation or in the deductive method of science. It is not my intention here to discuss the practical and conceptual merits of these methodologies as sources of knowledge. It is clear, however, that the viability of these procedures is a function of a *community* of people that share a particular form of communication.[6] Not the ideal communication or a dialogue but a communication *with* the other, nevertheless.

---

5 For a detailed explanation of this relation see Habermas (1990a) and also Freire (1999).

6 For an in-depth analysis of this relation see Habermas (1971).

And such community is fundamental for knowing reality. Its existence shows us that even when we do not recognize our human interdependence, interdependence is the condition of knowledge and, as such, it cannot be avoided.

The communication that excludes or a strategic communication, results from an unquestionable attachment to pre-validated social symbols and social roles. A strategic communication has other motives and goals than achieving mutual understanding. These motives are secured and perpetuated through external and internal restrictions that determine who can talk and what can be said and questioned. Demands that constitute a potential threat to the understanding, and consequent authority, of a particular way of life cannot be uttered or would be ignored. Dialogue, which structure is universal, can be only among those who recognize themselves equal in the process of knowing; among those who submit their self-assertion, established in solid reference to an unchangeable truth, to a self-understanding built in relationship with the other. This pattern of recognition built into dialogue engenders, in its turn, power relations that foster inclusion and diversity.

It is important to emphasize that the fact that each potential interlocutor is an equal in the process of understanding does not mean that our contributions to reaching agreement are the same "amount", in the hypothetical case this could be measured. Depending on what we are questioning, our information about it and the degree of our interest in questioning it may and will greatly vary. Dialogue, nevertheless, implies that the unconditional inclusion of the other will increase, for the moment at least, the correspondence of knowledge and action with the objective reality, with social justice and with one's own personal biography.

Dialogue and Human Unity

Dialogue implies the simultaneous recognition of a redeemable reality; of our own pre-understanding of this reality and of our mutual need in understanding it and implementing it as a true and just action. Based on these assumptions we can say that dialogue as the ongoing collective process of validating the truth, the justice and the sincerity of individual and group decisions is a reflection of human unity, at the same time that it promotes such unity.

The temporary agreement that participants reach in dialogue on the best course of action reveals the purpose of mutual recognition. In dialogue the need for recognition releases itself from the limitations of self-preservation and is finally directed towards self-understanding. Dialogue, by promoting an unrestricted questioning of all spheres of human understanding – otherwise limited to the requirements of personal and community preservation – reveals the true value of the self in a continuous and ever more complete manner.

In dialogue, recognition cannot be granted *a priori* to an already pre-validated understanding. Every claim that is raised has to convince every other interlocutor that it corresponds to everyone's perception of the world, including the perception of the non-modern interlocutor who enters dialogue with the initial claim, for instance, that the natural world is one with or is affected by the subjective inner reality of the knower.

Likewise, the claims of normative correctness cannot be validated only on the basis of the "validity surplus"[7] current within a particular society. Dialogue gives rise to a new validity surplus, the result of the overlapping claims of justice of all potential interlocutors, that is, all the communities and peoples of the world. A claim cannot be validated in dialogue on the basis that one or another or, as a matter of fact, several communities, have acted and enacted a set of norms and traditions for centuries or millennia. Such claim by itself is not redeemable for those who understand these actions as unfair, not necessarily as an injustice that is directly committed against them but as a practice that is against their own surplus of validity. In dialogue, every action, regardless of its local or global scope of influence, must redeem its value within the continuously transforming horizon of a universally agreed "surplus of validity".

Finally, the claims of sincerity or that one is acting without deceitful intentions, which is also the most challenging claim to be redeemed in a world characterized by a history of deceptions and increased lack of mutual trust, has to be validated by friends and foes alike. While in strategic communication only those who are *already* trustworthy are included as equal partners in the process of validation, dialogue approximates participants to the true intentions of each other because claims have to be redeemed by everyone, even by those who have been in the past or still find themselves in the present deceived by these claims.

For the above reasons, dialogue is a means for a purpose other than granting social recognition to participants and preserving patterns of thought and action. Within dialogue, recognition is unconditional – everyone is allowed therein, regardless of the social symbols that each participant holds. Because dialogue is built on this unconditional relation or on moral recognition, we say that dialogue is the *expression* of the inalienable condition of human unity and that it also *promotes* this condition or the collective self-understanding of those who partake in it. Unity tells us that self-understanding can never be an individual achievement. It tells us, in other words, of our non-contingent interdependency in the *search* for a contingent understanding. Dialogue, in its turn, is the only process through which this non-contingency gains expression. Outside dialogue, unity is a truthful promise, a constant search that, deprived of its means of expression, cannot come to fruition.

The contingent changes undertaken by human societies have eventually determined a unique set of circumstances for the actualization of dialogue and human unity. Though this has been an intuition and a certainty for some, and for thousands of years perhaps,[8] the material conditions and the patterns of thought required for the fulfillment of unity were not available as they are today. In other

---

7   I am using the term as used by Axel Honneth in Fraser and Honneth (2003).

8   See Heater (1996).

words, the practical conditions for an actual universal dialogue did not exist, in spite of the fact that dialogue had also for long been identified as the path to truth. Though human unity and its demand for dialogue are not recently "discovered" realities, dialogue can, for the first time, not only imply, but also be actualized as universal communication. Never before could the truth be assessed universally, as "universal" was limited to those surrounding neighbors who knew each other. And among those who knew each other, only a small group was recognized as an equal and thus allowed to participate in dialogue.

The equality of all human beings, a *sine qua non* condition of dialogue is a very recent pattern of thought. Without it there are no grounds to justify universal participation. If the other is not seen as a human, the *demand* to include him would not be possible, much less his actual inclusion. Events like the European maritime expansions that told all the communities of the earth of each other's existence; the successful struggles for recognition of previously excluded social groups; and the modern technology that creates the means that make communication among peoples possible; are all developments that have been fundamental for the actualization of dialogue. And this is what defines the uniqueness of our time. It allows for an unprecedented knowledge of truth, an unparalleled justice in decision-making processes and an unmatched release of individual potentialities.

Up to now truth and justice could only be partially understood, as most people would not be allowed in giving and demanding reasons to one another's claims. Today even if this participation is still difficult and very limited, due to the asymmetries and antagonisms that characterize prevailing power structures, the grounds necessary for the demand and actualization of universal participation in dialogue are established and agreed on. Dialogue can finally be actualized according to its own precepts because inequality, though still a characteristic of dominant power, can no longer be validated.

While for modernity power could be at the service of truth only if truth was reduced to what power *already* knew and allowed for, from the perspective of human unity the expansion of understanding challenges established power structures and re-direct them towards the *search* for truth. The modern reduction of truth created a mere servant for power. In the cases when understanding is simply pre-determined, power, however, is of no meaningful use to the beholder. It becomes a self-serving force, unresponsive and destructive and eventually removed by force. Conversely, when power is at the service of truth, that is, committed with fostering processes of understanding, power is responsive to *everyone*'s interests. A democratic regime, for instance, is safeguarded to the extent that it allows unity to be understood through the functioning of its institutions but it cannot, conversely, be protected with the institutional imposition of the value of human unity.[9]

A regime that expects its members' alliance because it protects a substantial truth or the true interests of people is *already* pre-determining these interests and legitimizing its own authority on the basis of such protection. Although power

---

9   For a similar discussion see Habermas (1998).

structures affect and can foster understanding, they can only do so to the extent that they are detached from particular power representations. Because reality is never in need of protection or preservation, on the contrary, it is powerful in itself, when power seeks to preserve the truth it is replaced by another power structure and representation that a different level of understanding has determined.

When power is not afraid of having its main claims questioned, by those who agree and equally disagree with them, it is protected, not necessarily against disintegration, but against corruption. An incorruptible power is not threatened by other powers because it does not need to assert any particular truth. It only has to create the conditions needed for the constant discovery and re-discovery of truth. And in this process it may well have to give way to other representations of power, to another political regime and authority. It will do so, however, not because, in a battle of powers, it lost to another more able to impose its truths or more "truthful" than itself. An incorruptible power changes because in its commitment with the search for truth a new understanding of reality demanded practical changes. More frequently than not, however, it is the new understanding that forcefully replaces the corrupt power with a power that is *temporarily* more responsive to everyone's interests, that is, less confrontational and more inclusive than the previous one.

Dialogue and the Development Debate

In the struggle between power and truth that is carried within the development debate, the truth is reduced to the struggle for self-preservation and put, in this way, at the service of that power that succeeded in preserving itself. The truth of poverty and freedom that the discourse of development sustains and the power of global development that it propagates is the struggle to spread all over the world particular means of self-preservation. The claim of antidevelopmentists to the right of the community to determine its own destiny represents, on the other hand, the struggle to secure the power that each community has to survive. Although antidevelopmentists argue for the coexistence of parallel powers, their claims to the truth are directed, nevertheless, to the legitimization of those powers that have been locally most successful in preserving the truth and themselves.

When truth is understood as a function of dialogue or dialogue is acknowledged as the condition of possibility of understanding, the relationship between power and truth changes. The status of truth does not have to be undermined so that a diversity of power representations can flourish nor has truth to be safeguarded against dissent in order to be powerful. When truth is determined in dialogue, antagonistic power structures give way to cooperative structures and power representations are diversified. Because those who engage in dialogue allow for the questioning of their claims, they overcome the exclusionist power structure that was needed to protect these claims.

Power at the service of understanding accepts other life styles not for the sake of avoiding a clash of powers, out of fear of the other's unknown power.

Its acceptance is out of understanding human unity as the condition that sustains power itself. Since truth has to be known with the universal other, the truth claims that power raises have to be redeemed within universal relations. Any power, but especially the one that is aware of its commitment with the search for truth, is maintained on the promise and possibility of this universal and all-inclusive redemption. And it disintegrates at the moment that such promise is proven impossible for that particular power.

The clash of powers that antidevelopmentists try to overcome by undermining the status of truth can only be overcome in dialogue. If there are no redeemable truths then power has no precepts and demands to respond to. In this case the truths that power protects, protecting itself in return, becomes the end towards which the exercise of power is directed. If such truths require the exercise of a global power in order to be protected, then for the precise reason that there is no possibility of mutual understanding and agreement, this power is legitimized in its efforts and eventual success.

The power of different societies, that is, society's structures and institutions, cannot as a matter of fact be preserved. In dialogue also they are unequivocally altered, as the truth claims raised by each society are questioned and reviewed. When different powers engage in dialogue, however, change does not reflect unequal power relations but the symmetrical structure of a dialogical relation. Dialogue overcomes the opposition between powers not because it starts an impartial and fair game where competitors do not know beforehand the end result or which power and truth will eventually survive and which will not. Dialogue is the only alternative to antagonistic power relations because it engages the sides in a relation where each contributes to the fulfillment of the common purpose of all.

Conflicting power representations have the option of searching for truth through all-inclusive relations of dialogue or to continue the struggle to preserve one's truths, feeding into the cycle of confrontation and self-destruction. It is important to stress that there is no third possibility for power relations, as antidevelopmentists deceivingly presents us: *preserving* one's local truths and at the same time not having to fight for them. In this sense, state sponsored military interventions and terrorist and guerrilla actions are more coherent in the means they use to achieve an eventually "peaceful" coexistence than intellectuals discursively advocating the nonexistence of truth.

The only thing that could possibly stop the cycle of aggression and destruction is precisely what antidevelopmentists have destroyed in their discourse. And, as such, antidevelopmentists end up defending the rights of "their" people for the same reason that the most dedicated developmentists do: compassion for the weaker. Compassion for those who will inevitably be destroyed if the stronger decides to use its power. And over and over, the question remains unanswered: why should the stronger limit its force? If the reason is actually compassion, let us then at least be coherent in our demands and do not claim for justice, respect to people's diversity or the protection of community's right to self-determination. Let us use the correct terms and ask for pity, mercy or charity. And if these reasons end up appealing to the stronger, all the better; but if they do not, then we will have to deal with the violent consequences of our normative mistake.

Like the futile effort of antidevelopmentists to preserve different powers by invalidating the truth, development's claim to know the truth paradoxically denies the power of truth. When development unilaterally stands for freedom, human rights, security and happiness, it is demanding support for an arbitrary power that will not hesitate, moreover, to destroy those who are not willing to cooperate with their "own" freedom. Ideas like freedom, happiness and prosperity become powerless – because not redeemable – and, in sheer contradiction with the people's empowerment that development seeks to promote, are used to justify arbitrary and non-responsive exercises of power. We are all too familiar with expressions of this process as Western nations' claim for development and universal human rights ironically reverts into exploitation and destruction of people's lives and livelihood.

The promise of substantial truth can just be made by a power that is at its own service and will seek to maintain itself without any concern for impoverishing and sacrificing the truths that it supposedly defends. Power that is submitted to truth cannot make any substantial promise; it can only grant the means for understanding. In spite of apparent lack of commitment and maybe unreasonable detachment, when power, expressed in social structures and institutions, works in this manner it fulfills the most basic requirement for the exercise of individual and collective choice. When these requirements are in place no other promises are needed to support and legitimize established authority. To promise anything else would be in fact to predetermine the object of human search and force him to live accordingly.

When power protects a particular truth, understanding and choice give way to a growing number of arbitrary assertions that determine what the truth is, what are its requirements and the consequences for disrespecting it. Norms and patterns of behavior and social institutions grow inflexible and intolerant as they benefit from an exercise of power tailored to the consolidation of truth. This does not mean that power, as the guardian of truth, is not ready to face charges of falling short from protecting its truths. Although such charges may seem to weaken the established power, it only confirms what power has been saying all along – everyone is in need of it – further legitimizing its authority. Power relations can change with these charges but power structures are never threatened by not fulfilling their promises.

What constitutes a disintegrating threat to power as the guardian of truth is the question of how meaningful and how valuable its promises are. This questioning is possible when the level of understanding within a social group is such that it is able to identify the socially dominant criteria for validating understanding and knowledge, other concomitantly available, though maybe not institutionalized, criteria and the inconsistencies between the two. When questions arise about truth, justice and true intentions which cannot be addressed by the prevailing power, authority loses legitimacy and power structures together with power relations change. It is for this precise reason that power structures committed with their own maintenance, will *assert* by every available means the validity of their claims, while delegitimizing and impeding the questioning of this validity. Contrary to truth claims that can be validated and thus also invalidated, power cannot. Clash and confrontation is the only means of sustaining monological power, regardless of how peaceful its claims and intentions might be.

It is important to emphasize that questioning the truth that power stands for has practical consequences that fundamentally differ from demanding that power fulfils its promises. Simply denouncing the discrepancy between what a society says and what it does, that is, identifying the surplus of validity within each society informs us of the extent that power is not promoting the equal distribution of a particular pattern of recognition, alongside with the material redistributions associated with this recognition. Such complain, by itself, cannot weaken a political or social order. It will actually come to its rescue as it points to the changes this regime has to undergo in order to secure the legitimacy of its structure.

What can result from this questioning is at best a change in power relations. But this is a change that maintains the same unquestioned and supposedly evident truth and, therefore, the same confrontational and exclusionist power structure. Adjustments in power done on these terms can never make a power less oppressive than it is. It can never, in other words, guarantee anything but survival or a social order where its members recognize and value each other for imitating the same established patterns of recognition. And as long as people's demand is to have a higher share of the benefits of power – afraid of losing the protection of power and with it the only self that power has allowed them to know – this recognition is all they will be able to give and receive from each other. Deluding themselves and justifying their support to a regime because it stands for their true interests, people will eventually have a society that equally and indiscriminately distributes its oppression.

Power can only be liberating when people question the value and meaning of power's premises. Through such questioning people's true interests are gradually known and the social and political order that these interests need to be materialized are re-created. This questioning happens when people do not accept to reduce their interests to only what their particular societies have to offer, that is, when they recognize each other for the role that each has in fostering mutual understanding. And it can only happen through dialogue, a non-exclusionist and non-antagonist power structure that denounces every power that seeks to justify itself through the preservation of truth.

In the age of globalization, dialogical power can and must answer to the actual demands of everyone. As people's claims today *can* be universally validated, that is, they can *also* constitute the experience of practical power, dialogical power *has* to be global in its scope. Truth claims raised everywhere have to be globally validated. In other words, every claim has to be answerable to everyone's demand for understanding. Giving and demanding reasons to one another, engaging in dialogue, becomes people's fundamental right in the age of globalization. Dialogue, in its turn, is the only means for respecting and promoting people's diversity, also fulfilling in this way the intended benefit that the development debate seeks when equating every human activity with a relative value.

Dialogue, Values and Globalization

If before globalization communities that were away from each other could understand and give meaning to their life styles without *practical* enrollment in universal dialogue, this cannot be achieved anymore. In order to live up to one's truth, enrolling in universal dialogue is an imperative. It is not so only because outside a multicultural dialogue survival is threatened, in a world where diverse and conflicting powers struggle for self-assertion. Dialogue is an imperative because above and beyond the challenges posed externally to one's survival, the new encounters pose a challenge to communities' self-understanding.

When we understand, even though initially only partially, the claims of other people and communities, not to ask them about our *own* truths is to start reproducing these truths for the sake of survival alone. Until the moment that we are not aware of the existence of a different other, what we do inside our communities may represent higher levels of self-understanding. When we encounter the other, however, what we do will cease to promote self-understanding and be reduced to self-preservation unless we include him in the validation of our truths. Refusing to do so because he is an outsider who lives by another set of truths is, at the precise moment of exclusion, a refusal to ask about the value of one's *own* truths. The exclusion reduces an ongoing process of self-understanding into the preservation of a self-relation that is threatened as previous understandings are faced with new ones.

The encounter of peoples and communities which asks for dialogue is not simply the imposition of an additional burden on everyone's shoulders. Dialogue represents the possibility of an expanded understanding of truth and justice, an understanding that releases human action from the burdens of imitation of socially accepted patterns of thought and behavior, fostering the realization of a new and diverse set of individual and group capacities. The dialogue that is stirred by globalization expands local possibilities; it gives people that have been sharing the same truths for generations the opportunity to reassess their truths and the unique value of their capacities.

The globalization process represents the practical possibility of communicating with another culture in equality. If we engage with each other in these terms we begin a process of self-understanding and self-realization. If we choose not to do so, on the other hand, there can be no awareness of the meaning and value of human diversity. There will be the classification of differences, as developed and underdeveloped, educated and ignorant, but these differences tell nothing meaningful about those who have been thus classified.

In dialogue, our singularity gains practical expression, social value and personal meaning. We not only become aware of how different we are but we also give new meaning to what would otherwise be an arbitrary difference. Our diversity thrives and becomes meaningful and valuable as it tells others about their uniqueness. The protection and fostering of everyone's diversity – irreplaceable precisely in what it represents for the fulfillment of every other diversity – becomes thus each one's concern and purpose. Retrieving the example of the human body, we can say that when the hand and the feet find out about each other, the meaning of what they did up to then and the possibility of what they can do in the future is transformed. It is changed in a way that allows both to better understand and fulfill their capacities. As a result it is in the best interest of the hand to protect the unique contributions of the feet to the body as it is of the feet to protect the hand's irreplaceable contributions to the whole.

Today we are living in a world where all the members of the body have the possibility to finally know about the singularity of one another and fulfill it without practical impediments. The global encounter of peoples and communities demands a new and challenging step towards the expression of our unique value: the inclusion of those whose existence was up to now ignored and, as a result, the inclusion of the familiar one also under new terms and conditions, that is, dialogical terms.

What still remains to be asked and pondered in the context of the globalization process, before I continue with the reflection of development as dialogue, is what kind of organization dialogue calls for. How are those who engage in dialogue to practically recognize each other, since traditional qualifications, dichotomous by nature, cannot serve as a basis for the mutual recognition of those who dialogue? Is there a particular mode of social organization that better reflect these relations of recognition? Does the new pattern of recognition ask for a global society, similar to what development project tries to promote or will local forms of social organization do more justice to it?

It is important to reflect on the implications of dialogue for social organization because organizational issues have been systematically evoked and challenged in the development debate, evidenced in the growing popularity of terms like "community building" and "grassroots movement". As we will see, the distinctive nature of the relations of recognition that dialogue requires are not expressed in the global society that developmentists stand for nor in the traditional forms of community organization that antidevelopmentists advocate. Dialogue can only be carried within a community of universal friendship, a form of organization the like of which is scarcely witnessed around the world and within modern and traditional societies alike.

Chapter 7
The Community of Friends

So far I have been talking about development in procedural terms, re-defining it as a dialogical process and explaining why this process overcomes social oppression, fosters people's diversity and expands self-understanding. But as a relation of recognition what is the type of practical association that dialogue fosters? This question is fundamental in the context of the development debate because the debate presents human relations as possible only within two seemingly distinct forms of organization, both of which are incompatible with the condition of human unity.

Antidevelopmentists explain the possibility of meaningful associations inside the context of shared symbolical experiences. For them, moreover, only the consolidation of this common background of values and traditions can offer a resistance and protection against the invasive and destructive power of modernity and development.[1] Developmentists, on the other hand, talk of the possibility of global relations based on universalizable norms. They claim that a set of norms and regulations on social coexistence can be universalized – norms on human rights, environmental safety and the free-market, for instance – to guarantee each society the maximization of its own interests. Although they argue that these are neutral in regards to local patterns of recognition, it is clear that, historically speaking, modernization followed by economic globalization has altered the very way that societies and communities value their local achievements and their members.

Despite differences in the procedure and practical organization of human affairs, both these relations represent a commitment with a substantial way of life that excludes the other in his universality. This exclusion overlooks the *a priori* of the universal other, which makes any particular relation of recognition, global or communitarian, a possibility. If this original and unconditional relation or agreement demands to be fulfilled in every other interaction, then only a type of association that reveals through its own structure this universal agreement can fulfill the particular and concrete purposes of each relation. If dialogue, as I want to argue, is what best expresses this agreement, then the above question on what would be the practical type of association that dialogue can foster would take

---

1   See, for instance, Howard (1995) and Esteva (1996).

us back to dialogical relations themselves, showing us that more than situational clarity we need in fact structural definitions.

In order to build my argument in this way I will begin with the idea that the original agreement or pact that constitutes human relations carries with itself a *promise* that is called into fulfillment whenever people come together and abide by a common life of norms and values, at different social scales. This original pact that precedes every other can be named, as we will see, a relationship of friendship. The more we respect it or relate as friends, by engaging in dialogical relations, the more the particular relation we chose to foster becomes meaningful. Similarly, the less we respect it, the more meaningless and oppressive these relations become, no matter whether locally or globally institutionalized.

The community of friends is more inclusive than the antidevelopmentists' community and more diverse and substantial in its possibilities than the supposedly neutral global society of developmentists. It addresses a communitarian and a universal condition of human relations that is not addressed by either side in the development debate. To understand why this is so and how dialogue expresses this community and pursues the promise within it, let me start, aided by the work of Jacques Derrida on the same subject, with a reflection on the cosmopolitan nature of friendship.

Defending at once a cosmopolitanism and a community life that are in contrast with the liberal discourse on universalism as well as with the antidevelopment argument for community, Mark Bevir (2001) defines in the following terms the characteristics of a "Derridean" cosmopolitanism:

> Before any allegiance to a particular group, we belong to a cosmopolitan community. ... Although we have our being only in common with those others with whom we share a life-world, there is an Other that comes 'before' our existential relationship to these others. ... Even as we recognize the importance of others in constructing our life-world, so we inevitably open the space of the Other understood as that which remains outside of the shared life-world we thus evoke. (126–127)

This Other that is not the one we know, who does not have a proximity to our being but still is the condition of possibility of a relation with the particular others we know, determines a cosmopolitan responsibility to every person regardless of his culture or life style, that is, *a response that is first to an understandable call and then to the caller*:

> The concept of the Other sets up a cosmopolitan responsibility prior to any commitment to a shared identity or common enterprise. ... his [Derrida's] insistence on the importance of difference (of recognizing how any present is bound up with an absent) entails a stress on the inherent limitations of all attempts to postulate a particular culture as that which binds us to the relevant others. (Bevir 2001: 128)

It is not culture what binds us to one another, that is, what has a concrete existence and has *already* been materialized. But what binds us together is that which makes culture possible in the first place:

> To reify a culture is to set up an apparently simple presence without recognizing the place of what is absent; it is to force the fact of difference into a myth of sameness; it is to collapse the ethical Other into existential others. (Bevir 2001: 128)

The solution to this reification of culture, the forceful identities and the arbitrary exclusions that it creates is to *intentionally* adopt a cosmopolitanism that is open to the Other:

> We must respect singularity in a way that asks of us an openness to alterity. We must acknowledge an ethical relationship prior to our membership of any particular group, a relationship that does not depend upon the other holding certain beliefs, recognizing given authorities, performing a set of actions, belonging to a particular race, living in a certain neighborhood, or speaking a given language. (Bevir 2001: 128–129)

On the other hand, this cosmopolitanism stands far from the global society that development discourse justifies and the requirements of self-maintenance that development project seeks to impose:

> Because liberals generally are wedded to individualism, they tend to adopt a universalism based on a vision of how individuals should come together. They postulate a set of rights that individuals, or perhaps cultures, acquire by virtue of entering global society, or they explore the global norms on which all individuals, or perhaps cultures, can agree. (Bevir 2001: 133)

Cosmopolitanism differs from this liberal universalism as it:

> Does not consist of agreed norms or a set of rights so much as a reminder of the ethical stance or responsibility to others that follows from this fact of community. This responsibility moves us from an artificial, even imperialistic, construction of consensus, or agreed norms, to an openness to alterity. *It moves us from a duty of respecting the right of others to a gift of friendship to the Other.*[2] (Bevir 2001: 134)

While addressing what we would call here the antidevelopment discourse on community, Bevir argues for the recovery of the universal Other, which every

---

2   Emphasis added. For a comprehensive discussion on Cosmopolitanism see Derrida (2003).

established community implies. When he responds to modern and liberal forms of universalism, which is implied in the development discourse, he recovers not the rights of the universal other and the duty to respect them but the gift of his friendship. The universal Other is in reality absent from both discourses and the friendship we can offer to one another what is missing in both practices. Remembering this other and recovering this friendship it is what any proposal for more just and meaningful relationships can and should do.

Derrida recovers the original pact of friendship in the "undeniable future anterior", a perfect relationship that is at the beginning and at the end of human relations but it is not at the present and, therefore, a relation towards which we have to work. Still, as a perfect relation, friendship can "never be given in the present; it belongs to the experience of waiting, of promise, or of commitment".[3]

The "undeniable future anterior" that is the time of friendship is derived from the fact of language and what makes understanding possible. According to Derrida we can understand each other because we have already shown each other friendship, which he defines as

> this preliminary consent without which you would not understand me, would not listen to my appeal, or be sensitive to what is hopeful in my cry. Without this absolute past, I could not be together in a sort of minimal community – but one which is also incommensurable with any other – speaking the same language or praying for translation within the horizon of the same language, even were it so as to manifest a disagreement, if a sort of friendship prior to friendship, an ineffaceable, fundamental, and bottomless friendship, the one that draws its breath in the sharing of a language (past or to come) and in the being-together that any allocution supposes, including a declaration of war. (636)

Like Derrida, who justifies the simultaneous ideal and anteriority of friendship reconstructing the conditions that make mutual understanding through the use of language possible, I want to recover this friendship within relations of mutual recognition which are constitutive of human relations and associations at every scale, local and global. My intention, like Derrida's, is to justify the original precedence of friendship in human relations and, in this way, to legitimize the expectation and the demand that friendship be practiced in the actuality of our daily interactions.

The need for recognition determines that every kind of relation, what we look for in each one of them, is valuable and desirable not for itself but for the recognition of the other that such relation promises. Every ethical recognition assumes in this way an anterior moral recognition. Every ethical recognition, mediated and conditioned by the particular symbols of each community, is the search for an unconditioned recognition of an honest and, therefore, universal other. This original or moral recognition, although always present, has to be

---

3   Derrida 1988: 636.

remembered if we are to fulfill that which we are looking for in our daily and even most dirempted relations. A community can only foster the positive self-relation of its members, in terms of and expanding self-understanding, if it fosters patterns of recognition that do not exclude the universal other.

Implied in the *a priori* of moral recognition is a relation of universal friendship. Friendship denounces and re-orients the search for community, on the one hand, and the protection of universal human rights, on the other, re-affirming not only its "undeniable future anterior" but also the ideal of a practical global community of friends. But before undertaking this analysis it is important to clarify what I mean by friendship. The *meaning* of friendship is initially inferred from the identification of the *purpose* of every human relation with the pursuit of friendship.

The most current understanding of friendship, the one that prevails in people's imaginary, in general, and in the development debate, in particular, is of Aristotelian background. Aristotle equated friendship with dearness and argued that only those people or things that are familiar to us can be dear. He, furthermore, identifies three sorts of dear of lovable things: the good, the pleasant and the useful. In order for friendship to exist these three conditions have to be given between those who already know each other and are aware of each other's disposition. It can be said, otherwise, that there is unilateral goodwill or well disposition in regards to the other but not friendship. Friendship is, therefore, the pleasure, utility or the good that each represents to the other. Two kinds of friendship, those based on utility and pleasure, are accidental because the friends do not love each other in themselves but "in so far as some benefit accrues to them from each other" Aristotle (1996): 207. Friendship of this kind can be easily broken because the other is only loved for what he has to offer to one's own pleasure.

Only one form of friendship is perfect so that those who love each other can call themselves friends in the fullest sense. This is the friendship between those who are good. Since the good is what is loved and good people are good or virtuous in themselves, those who love the good wish the good of their friends for their friends sake and not for what the friend gives them in return. This perfect friendship does not exclude the other two forms of friendship, since the good friend is also a pleasant and useful one, but it goes beyond them in terms of permanence and its absolute nature. Its absolute nature implies that the other types of friendship have their existence defined in relation to this one or that they are imperfect forms of this only real form of friendship. Aristotle eventually argues that this type of friendship is very rare and happens between those few people who are good and even then only after a long time spent in intimacy:

> as the saying goes, you cannot get to know a man till you have consumed the proverbial amount of salt in his company; and so you cannot admit him to friendship or really be friends, before each has shown the other that he is worthy of friendship and has won his confidence. People who enter into friendly relations quickly have the wish to be friends, but cannot really be friends without

being worthy of friendship, and also knowing each other to be so; the wish to be friends is a quick growth, but friendship is not. (Aristotle 1996: 209)

Friendship from this perspective, and specially a perfect friendship, seems to be incompatible with the possibility of friendship with the universal other, a friendship which exists even before we enter into a concrete relationship with him. We can rightly wonder how are we, even if accepting the *a priori* of a certain friendship or the "desire to be friends", work for the promotion of a global community of friends, should we have to consume a "proverbial amount of salt" in the company of one another before we may know the goodness and befriend each other. This is especially the case when one thinks that, although the utility and the pleasure of a relation may be more readily available for mutual assessment and agreement, the goodness that the other personifies may be the function not only of time spent together but of early forms of socialization that cannot be translated from one life style to another.

Plato may help us here with this reflection. He defines friendship in terms of that first principle for the sake of which everything else is dear. Everything, says Plato, is dear for the sake of something else. Proceeding in this way we shall arrive at

> Some first principle of friendship or dearness which is not capable of being referred to any other, for the sake of which, as we maintain, all other things are dear, and having there arrived we shall stop. (...) My fear is that all those other things, which, as we say, are dear for the sake of another, are illusions and deceptions only, but where that first principle is, there is the true ideal of friendship. (1956: 27)

Plato does not define the content of this first principle. He only says that friendship should be sought in reference to this ideal:

> And although we may often say that gold and silver are highly valued by us, that is not the truth; for there is a further object, whatever it may be, which we value most of all, and for the sake of which gold and all our other possessions are acquired by us. ... That which is only dear to us for the sake of something else is improperly said to be dear, but the truly dear is that in which all these so-called dear friendships terminate. And the truly dear or ultimate principle of friendship is not for the sake of any other or further dear. ... Then we have done with the notion that friendship has any further object. [We may then infer] that the good is the friend. (1956: 28)

Plato, like Aristotle, recognizes different levels of friendship and both speak of one highest form of friendship from which the other ones are derived. While Aristotle, however, defines perfect friendship in terms of the good, Plato argues that it is the true friend who determines what the good is. In Aristotle's work it becomes clear that the embodiment of a substantial good is what defines true friends. For Plato it is the friend, dear in himself, and *whatever* he embodies, that tells us about the good. While for Aristotle relations built on goals that are not good are illusions, for Plato it is friendship itself – and not the good – that has no further object. One could conclude that for Plato the illusion would be to think that the good can determine true friendship, while every substantial good is in reality dear only because of a previous friendship.

Political philosophers have extensively explained that the good, defined in Aristotelian terms, can only belong to the way of life of individual communities or to the individual choices of free citizens. That is why, for instance, Aristotle could say that "the actions of all good men are the same or similar" (1996: 209). They have also argued that the good cannot be universalized. Although liberal philosophers argue that there are universalizable procedures that are neutral in regards to the substantial choices of social groups – and could for this reason foster a peaceful co-existence among these groups – communitarian and liberals both agree that substantial values cannot for the most part be cross-culturally translated.[4] Within this context, friendship as a function of the good or among the good people alone, could not justify and demand universal relations. It could only be among those who share the same concept of the good or hold the same things, thoughts or attitudes, as dear or loved.

It is less clear if the universalizable procedures or principles of justice claimed by liberals either imply or could result in a relationship of universal friendship. Although it could be argued, along with Plato, that a substantial agreement is not a necessary requirement of friendship – because any other good that serves this purpose, but the friend himself, is the illusion of those who have not found true friendship – it remains to be asked what beyond a shared ethical life, if anything, could determine the absolute, non-contingent or true dearness of the other. It would also be important to ask in this regard whether an agreement on the concept of good would result from a true relation of friendship.

The impossibility of a universal friendship is as part of the development discourse as it is of the antidevelopment discourse. The only difference is that in the first case friends do not have to belong to the same community as the good is an individual choice. In the second, true friendship occurs among members of the same community and the previous "liberal" friendship can only be one of utility or pleasure.[5] The fact that in both discourses, however, some type of friendship is more real and desirable than another reveals that friendship has a seemingly unavoidable structure. If I can show that this structure is implied in both sides' claims of what an ideal relationship ought to be, then the demand that this structure

---

4   For more recent discussions on the task of reconciling the good with the principle of fairness, a most challenging task that multicultural and democratic societies call for, see Rasmussen (1990), Gutman (2003), Walzer (2007) and Sandel (2010).

5   See, for instance, how Esteva and Prakash (1997) and Mies and Shiva (1993) criticize the social relations that development fosters.

be also respected in the actualization of these relations will be justified. I will next discuss this structure as I explore the question of an alternative pattern of mutual recognition for the peoples of the world, one that sets itself apart from both the reification of culture that antidevelopmentists undertake and from the intended neutrality and practical impositions set by the global development project.

Friendship in the Antidevelopment Discourse

For antidevelopmentists the friendship that modernity and development can promote is at best a conditional one, where the other will be strategically used as a means for achieving certain ends. This "liberal friendship" cannot be a true friendship, as the other can never be loved for the good that he holds or believes in. Because the good is a community construction, any kind of friendship outside the limits of the community is a friendship that necessarily happens for some other reason than sharing the same good and, therefore, instrumental in nature.

What is overlooked in this approach, however, is that whatever unites people in friendship has to be defined in terms of that first principle for the sake of which every other construction is dear. Otherwise, that friendship is instrumental and strategic. As such, this principle raises a claim that should hold as the best among all available claims, that is, as not refutable in face of all the other claims that are concomitantly raised. This means that by definition the good is not the arbitrary determination of locally successful power. Besides its contextual particularities, it also lends itself to universal redemption. As such, antidevelopmentists argument for a friendship that can only be built around a good that is confined to the limits of the community is as strategic as the relations that can be built within a global society. By defining the good *only* as a relative community construct, antidevelopmentists imply that the good should be dear simply because there is a community that had the power to determine it as so.

To love something only because one's community has produced it, without assuming that its value can be redeemed or that if it can, it is only partially, by select and pre-determined people, means that the good is that which forcefully guarantees the legitimacy of other community's claims and values – in other words, what guarantees the preservation and survival of the community. Antidevelopmentists are, in this way, putting friendship at the service of the unquestioned *preservation* of community symbols. And this is precisely what a friendship of utility that they would so readily criticize is: one that has the purpose of fostering other ends but the good.

When the first principle for the sake of which everything else is dear is the maintenance of the community, friendship exists only while all the sides are working to promote this end. As soon as the member of a community does not hold its symbols as dear, he is seen as the enemy of that community and it is justified for him to be punished, ostracized or banished.[6] The temporality, instrumentality and illusion of such communitarian friendship is as that of any trans-cultural, global or capitalist friendship. In the latter case, when the symbols of the liberal society are not hold dear by another this will also be excluded, marginalized or will suffer sanctions. In both cases what matters, nonetheless, is the survival of a particular way of life and only those who work for the *preservation* of the same ends can be friends.

Another co-related argument of the antidevelopment discourse that points out to the nature and structure of friendship is that global relations can only be instrumental because the *time* of friendship is missing therein. The argument is that people within such relations cannot be friends because they cannot possibly spend enough time together to learn about each other, to trust and eventually share a common understanding. The emphasis on a time that does not exist in global relations, however, does not undermine the possibilities of this relation, instead it re-enforces the universal quality of the good.

The time that is required for acquaintance with the other, for knowing whether the other is good and worthy of one's trust points to the nature of a good that cannot be immediately known. It is because the good that the other beholds and embodies is not self-evident that time is required before people can know each other as friends. Implied in the common sense that a stranger cannot simultaneously be a friend is the assumption that the good has a substantial content that makes itself only gradually known, that is, the good is not simply the imposition of victorious power. Sharing a common life, though it may be a prerequisite of friendship, is not its sufficient causation. Members of the same community would still have to spend considerable time together in order to become true friends. This is so because the good, although a community construction, is also unknown and has to be sought after. Friendship, therefore, takes time for two reasons: because we can never take for granted that the other embodies the good and because we are not, once and for all, absolutely sure what the good is.

We may choose to call the relations that antidevelopmentists and developmentists foster "true" friendship and embrace them as the best practical possibility for human relations. What cannot be consistently argued, however, is that the parties propose fundamentally different options or that the quality of one is superior to the other. Because both sides' core assumptions are the same, the friendship that is thereof made possible is not in one case more caring or less strategic than in the other.

It is my argument, nevertheless, that existing local and global relations can be improved and another kind of friendship is possible. This possibility is justified through the reconstruction of those conditions that make every practical friendship

---

6   See, for instance, how Esteva (1996) and Esteva and Prakash (1998) build their critique to the idea of universal human rights and development. The same legitimate exclusions are witnessed within other supposedly more modern and liberal collectivities, like political parties' or nation-states' severe punishment of "betrayers".

possible, that is, by questioning the structure of these friendships and understanding the horizon of possibilities that this structure unfolds.

In order to understand what other friendship is possible beyond the one bound to shared forms of life or individual interests, we should ask what is that makes any reality dear. We know that realities gain meaning and value within a community. So we may infer that the first principle of dearness is the "value attributing" community. Anything is dear or good as long as there is a community of people who attributes it such value, the thing having initially no dearness by itself. The universal principle that allows for any relative social good is, therefore, the recognition of the other.

But what if this value-attributing other is *a priori* restricted to only those who already hold a particular value? In this case, it would be correct to say that the first principle of dearness, the other, is being submitted to a secondary cause of dearness, an object which value is dependent on the first cause. For this reason if antidevelopmentists are to be coherent with their claim for a non-contingent friendship and with their critique that such friendship is not possible in development theory and practice, they cannot condition the other to any particular trait or attribute. It is a contradiction in principle to say that the other is the first cause of dearness only and as long as he thinks and acts in one way and not another. This other, who makes any social construct or value a possibility and is the measure of friendship, has evidently to be dear prior to any qualifications and, for this reason, a universal other. If his dearness consists in recognizing the value of a *particular* social construct, valuable as *already* a member of a community that subscribes to these social constructs, his so claimed unconditional value and the non-instrumentality of his friendship, is conditioned and submitted to what becomes in this case the unconditional value of social symbols. These social symbols, moreover, acquire an arbitrary existence. By placing friendship within community limits it is assumed that social symbols just happen to be, by mere chance or revelation, without communicable and understandable reasons to explain their existence.

Paradoxically, when the other is unconditionally dear or valued social symbols or a particular notion of good can be validated and thus be meaningful and valuable – non-arbitrary – for the beholder. Symbols are or become valuable because they express the capacity of a community and its members to create and attribute value to reality. If a symbol was an arbitrary construct, which did not reflect the original and creative capacities of a people, this symbol will have no value and its preservation will be meaningless. Likewise, though communities can give rise and constantly renew a wide variety of social symbols, these cannot be randomly discarded and forcefully replaced, without severe consequences for the self-relation of individuals and communities.

Symbols are meaningful because beyond the survival that they grant, they tell the community *how* it is surviving. They are the means through which a community asserts its capacity to survive. As such, no social symbol is arbitrary, its existence has a reason and a reason that will be unique for each community. This uniqueness reflects the singularity of each community or the singular way through which a community asserts its capacity to survive. Social symbols are valuable as long as they reflect the capacities of those who value it.

Recovering our initial question on what makes a reality dear, we can now add to our reflection that any reality is dear because of the existence of a community that is *capable* of valuing reality as such – and not simply because the community successfully remains. It is this creative capacity, which is, moreover, an original capacity for each community, what allows for something to be identified as dear or good.

The good, to the extent that it reflects unique capacities, is relative. No social good can be said to be of higher value than another because this would mean to compare qualities that share no common ground in relation to which they could be compared and assessed. Since they are unique, they are by definition, and in this regard only, also incomparable. Beyond its particularities, any relative good has, nevertheless, a universal character. This condition allows different conceptions of the good to question one another, and with this questioning to constitute the substance of friendship.

Social goods or symbols are for each and every community the expression of its search for self-understanding. They not only imply unique capacities but are also the *expression* of these capacities. The universal nature of the good consists in this, that it represents the universal process of *knowing* and *expressing* one's own capacities. The good, therefore, although incomparable in the particular capacity that it represents, has necessarily to represent people's expression of their capacities in order to be good. The implication of this argument is not that everything is good as long as there is a community that produces and supports it. The universal character of social goods has to be assessed by every relative good if this is to remain as such. To put it in another way, the condition of dearness of social symbols determines that these be universally assessed if they are to express and foster community's self-understanding.

Although what is dear and good for each people is unique, only that is dear which promotes higher levels of self-understanding. Nothing could be dear if it did not carry the promise of such ongoing achievement. In the absence of this promise, as we have already seen, not even a most instinctual reality as survival can be dear. Going back to the question of the first principle for the sake of which everything else is dear, we can say that this refers not only to successful patterns of mutual recognition – those that guarantee the permanence of a community in time – but to patterns of recognition that can foster the understanding and expression of one's original capacities.

True friendship can now be defined. It refers to that relation which allows its members to enroll in the process of self-understanding. Friends are those who remember the original source of their own value(s). They are those who do not deny the possibility of friendship in the name of particular values. Their interaction with one another is built on patterns of recognition that acknowledge their common and universal search. What they look for in one another is not support for the preservation of their goods but the possibility of understanding the meaning of these goods. In friendship the other cannot be temporarily or accidentally loved. He is loved in the non-contingent good that he represents. The good that *any* other represents and that makes everyone the perfect friend – even when we choose not to recognize a particular other as a friend and not take him into actual friendship – is the good of expanding our own self-understanding.

This good cannot be subtracted from anyone. It is not a temporary attribute or a quality that some could be deprived from or decide not to uphold. It is an attribute that is always present. True or non-illusory universal friendship is thus not a remote dream and, for this reason, an option. It is human condition itself, as for the subject there are "no further objects" than the unknown possibilities of recognition the other represents – be this other called a friend, an enemy, an excluded or downthrown. Because the only path to a cognizant or reflexive self-relation is this recognition, the other is unavoidably dear in himself, although through domination and exclusions we may try to manipulate and control this recognition. He is not loved for what he can offer or guarantee to the other but simply because he is the good that is loved by itself.

To our question of what is loved by itself, we could say that one's own self is the "dearest of them all". However, as love for the self is not only love to *have* a self but love to *know* this self and because knowledge is relational, the other is an absolute end. When we say that in true friendship the other *is* the good and cannot be used as a means to achieve another end, we are saying that the true friend is the one who tells us about our self. This is the highest good but a good that, in principle, is shared by everybody in equality, that is, their irreplaceability in telling us who we are.

The friend is loved for his own sake, for the absolute good that he *is* and not for a good that he temporarily *has* to offer. He is the only one who fosters self-understanding and this good is part of his condition. He is not a means for something else, valuable beyond himself. He is the absolute value from which every other value derives. When conversely we love somebody because and only as long as he or she shares with us the same relative goods, we are using the other's recognition to preserve our self. By detracting the other from his universality, that is, by denying the possibility of his unpredictable response, we are setting preservation as a self-sufficient goal and detracting from our relative goods any value that they would otherwise have. Friendship restricted to those who share the same values alone is a deviation from the search for understanding the meaning of these values and a struggle towards self-preservation.

The reverse reasoning is also correct. When the struggle for survival becomes the end, it requires the other to be a mere beholder of the means of survival. The friend cannot question either his role or these means. When we try to preserve our symbols, when we fear the death of a self-image which reasons we have not learned to question, the other can only be a temporary and accidental friend. He cannot be valued for his own sake because he is just the one that gives a pre-determined assent to a symbol, which gives the appearance of being dearer or more loved than he is. When the search for self-understanding is conditioned to the struggle for self-preservation, the other cannot be loved for who he fundamentally is. Any other, friend or foe can only be used according to the place where they stand and the symbols that they hold. A so called friend may seem dearer than the marginalized and excluded but those who condition their friendship to self-preservation, do not love anyone. One may well wonder whether the self-relation of the instrumentalized friend is in any better shape than the one whose friendship has been denied.

When a symbol is loved by itself it loses its meaning and its existence gives witness to only one aspect of our condition: our fear of death. Because the symbol is not loved for the creative self who values and gives meaning to it, it becomes a reality that has no unique and original reason to be preserved. It is preserved simply because it exists, because "it was already there when we arrived", because they were the only tools given to us to define and understand ourselves and we don't know what else could be and how to replace them. These symbols are constantly reproduced by a community of instrumental friendship that tells its members that they can only be friends as long as everyone's fear of losing the symbol is equally shared. But, of course, the question that we forget to ask is why do we look for the other's assent to our symbols? Why do we need him to be as afraid as we are of losing them? Perhaps because we don't fear losing the symbols to which we so tightly hold but losing the friendship of the other and, along with it, the sense of purpose that these symbols convey.

What we forget in instrumental friendship is precisely this aspect of our condition. We try to guarantee an equal dependency towards a symbol that is constantly threatening us with abandonment, not necessarily by changing hands – a less threatening and more remediable absence – but by losing its meaning. To face this abandonment we seek to force the other, sometimes "softly" and many times not, into the recognition of our material and non-material symbols. The artifacts that we use to keep the value of the symbol in place are less important for social critique than the route of power that we take to preserve meaning. The use of power, present every time that exclusions and inclusions are *pre-determined*, overlooks the condition of absolute symmetry that determines the value of social symbols. No one can, for this reason, force or use someone else to consent to meaning. Any time social relations are submitted to the preservation of symbols, the practical exclusions *and* inclusions that result thereof, deprives everyone, not necessarily of their symbols, but of meaningful ones. The lost happens at the very moment one tries to prevent it.

To exclude someone from the community of friends because he does not hold certain symbols is to reduce one's own value and dearness to the simple possession and preservation of these symbols. When we are aware that the fear of losing a symbol is the result of an anterior fear, a fear that comes from the possibility of a loss that is equally shared, there is no reason to condition the dearness of the other to his consent or embodiment of certain symbols. There is no need to try forcing dependency on the symbol as the measure of friendship. Because both sides are *equally* vulnerable to the loss of each other's absolute value, the use of force is self-defeating.

Knowledge of this symmetrical condition is crucial for overcoming social exclusions and instrumental friendship, that is, awareness that underlying these dirempted social relations is always an ideal friendship. True friendship, however, as Aristotle correctly points out but for the wrong reason, takes time after all. Though the longing for it is always present, an organic power that structures and propels daily relations forward, it also has to be intentionally sought after. The other is the ever present promise of self-understanding but not self-understanding itself. Self-understanding is in itself a *possibility,* never granted, always pointing to the horizon of what it is yet to come. Seeking the friendship of the other is holding unto this promise and possibility, not letting go of it because some relation or some people may have deceived us in the friendship that we sought.

The time that true friendship requires, therefore, is not the time of the future when the good of the other will be verified and confirmed, that is, the time that will tells us whether or not we can place in him our trust. The time of true friendship is the always present time of request and the time of answer. It is in the present that we might choose to deceive each other or renew our mutual trust, as we answer to each other's request for unconditional recognition in the search for the self. This is also not the time of the past, of certainties and irreversible exclusions. It is the time of renewal because every time we fail to offer an unconditional recognition we should be allowed to try again.

Although antidevelopment discourse claims an alternative form of relation and association that would supposedly be more meaningful for the participants, we saw why the recovery of community ties of friendship and solidarity cannot be more meaningful to community members. If these local relations are not built on the recognition of the universal other, power relations might change but the structure of oppression will remain intact. I will next explain why the so called universal individualism of the development project is equally unable to address the problem of meaninglessness and oppression. After this I will explain why a dialogical relationship alone, carried either in more local or global contexts, can represent and promote friendship and foster self-understanding and realization.

Friendship in the Development Discourse

In the development discourse, friendship is a rare, if ever seen, idea. Pushed out of the public life by the discourse of modernity in general, friendship has been relegated to the private life of individuals who are supposedly free to choose when and whom associate with in friendship. For this reason, friendship is not a requirement of development and the assessment of its possible benefits finds no place in the development discourse. Modern development proudly sustains that one's development is not, should not, be a function of how he is recognized by others, especially how he is recognized within the private sphere of the other's life.

Friendship loses its connection with development when it is made into a private choice and when development is so defined as not to render itself affected by exclusions from particular circles of mutual trust and dearness.

On the other hand, antidevelopmentists, as we have seen, are much more prone to talk in terms of friendship and its social benefits. For them, community is the locus of friendship and without a caring community no action can be taken or valuable for another. The community, and not private and individual relations, is the place where people are dear and supported, where they are cared for and protected and where they can build a solid and cohesive self-relation. To name any project or action taken outside this context "development" is, at best, a corruption of the term and, at worst, an evil invention, so much to render its use irrevocably oppressive.

The antidevelopment critique is not simply that development project is not neutral in regards to friendship preferences or that, contrary to what it claims, it has failed in freeing the technical and economic dimensions of human existence from its emotional and personal side. The argument is more comprehensive and profound than that. By ignoring friendship as an all permeating dimension of human experience, development theory and practice has also corrupted the idea and the possibility of friendship itself – the remaining refuge for the encounter and re-organization of social affairs. Relations ruled by the imperatives of capitalism and the maxim of personal profit reveals an instrumentalized other that cannot be suspended and restituted to a private *lifeworld* where the self will, temporarily, regain its integrity.

Modern liberal philosophers have systematically shown how capitalist societies perpetuate themselves by ingeniously and effectively invading and colonizing the changing elements of the *lifeworld*.[7] What they have been less keen to address, however, is the critique that the modern demand for the division between system and the *lifeworld* is, to begin with, a fragmentation in self-relation and that, moreover, the self can only be set free when this division itself is overcome. What these authors have not conjectured is the possibility that systems are effective in co-opting the private sphere not because of their own internal mechanisms but because the fragmented self strives for integration and "invades" the system, instead, with his own drives and requirements.

In a society ruled by capitalist maxims, the other is *socially* valued only as long as he contributes to economic growth. This *pre-determination* of value by the system signifies that no social protection, security and value can be given to him if he is not at least willing to support society in *this* way. When protection measures are taken, like the benefits granted by the welfare state, these are not for the sake of people themselves but for the imperatives of a political and economic order. The development discourse, however, more than a simple off-spring of the capitalist way of thinking, contains original elements through which it seeks to address the other not as a means but as an end in him or herself. The best

---

7   See Habermas (1990b) and Hartmann and Honneth (2006).

known and well-established among these are the arguments for the moral duty and social responsibility that the developed countries have towards the poor.[8] But as antidevelopmentists would correctly point out, social measures thus justified never require relations of mutual care and support, where the sides equally need and can, moreover, equally assist each other.[9]

While development is addressed to the underdeveloped, to those who are not able to provide for their own selves and need, therefore, the help of the more capable, antidevelopmentists argue that their alternative is for those who, in friendship, care for each other. The protection that the community offers, its safety networks, builds a positive self-relation and self-esteem. It tells community members about their diverse capacities and how these contribute to community life. The moral duty and social responsibility that developmentists, in good will, evoke, on the other hand, could not be further away from the requirements of true friendship and an integrated self. To recognize the other as temporarily devoid of practical capacity, undermining in this process the value of his social contributions along with his self-esteem, is what an enemy would do to another, not a friend. Social projects that ask "how can I help you?" do not alter the structure of oppression. Within the community of friends, the parties should concomitantly *ask* for help.[10]

It should be clear at this point in our discussion on human interdependency and on the symmetry of power relations that the claim that developed countries have a moral duty in regards to the "poor" and must display some form of social responsibility towards them falls short from the requirements of and the expected benefits of friendship. In other words, it cannot foster an integrated self-relation and growing inclusion. There is, however, another self-referential and non-instrumental claim in the development discourse, which is related to the previous one and that has to be analyzed before development project can be altogether ruled out as a viable alternative for meaningful social relations and positive self-relation.

Though not devised within the context of friendship, the discourse of universal human rights, through which development, among other means, legitimizes its actions, addresses the other in terms of the absolute value that he represents. In the development discourse respect to universal human rights is used to justify and demand development strategies that reduce absolute and relative poverty and inequality. In other words, the "right to development", as it has become commonly accepted,[11] invest the wealthy with the moral duty and the responsibility to develop the world.

---

8   See Singer (2009) and Yunus (2007), for instance.

9   See Illich, et al. (2005).

10   See Illich (1992), Rahnema (1992) and Illich, et al. (2005).

11   See Frankovitz (2002), Nowak (2002), McNeill and StClair (2009) and Sarkar (2009) for an analysis of the Article I of the 1986 UN Declaration on the Right to Development and UNESCO's case for understanding 'poverty as a violation of human rights'.

Respect to human dignity – the final object of the human rights discourse, broadly defined in terms of individual and collective freedom of choice – starts with what development strategies can afford.[12] This is not to say that authors have not looked at this picture from the other way around. Disrespect to non-economic universal human rights could also represent a threat to economic development and its goals.[13] From this perspective:

> The positive linkage between human rights and development cooperation plays ... a much more important role in the policies of bilateral and multilateral development agencies than the negative approach of human rights conditionality. The positive linkage means that donor countries started to use development cooperation funds for programmes and projects aimed at promoting human rights and democratization. (Nowak 2002: 19)

Generally speaking, the proponents of a necessary interdependency between development and human rights acknowledge that this is a bilateral process. Not only have human rights been redefined but the conceptualization of development and poverty has also been broadened within this newly "unraveled" unity.[14] Regardless of how one chooses to look at it, this has been a win-win arrangement for both discourses and set of practices.

Not everyone, however, is as optimistic about these possibilities. More than concern about whether poverty, narrowly or more comprehensively defined, is a violation of human rights, there is the reasonable apprehension as to how such language colonizes and threatens the potential of the human rights discourse to empower communities against various forms of globalization and economic domination and exploitation, that is, against development itself[15]:

> market concepts like privatization, liberalization and deregulation are now also considered as prerequisites for human rights. Human rights seem to have been taken-over by the dominant market rationality, which has led to ... the *marketization* of human rights. (Onazi 2009: 2)

From the perspective of those who criticize this fusion of discourses and ideas, development as a human right is the universalization and prioritization of certain rights above others and the regulation of nation-states' internal and external affairs according to these priorities. Besides the right to sovereignty and self-determination, which universality seems unproblematic to the critics, the question that eventually results from these reflections is whether there are any universal

---

12 See Uvin (2004), Pogge (2008), Hafner-Burton (2009) and Chong (2010).
13 See Hamm (2001), Nowak (2002) and Goldsmith (2007).
14 Hamm 2001.
15 See also Garcia (1999).

rights in the face of which discourses of "failing sovereignty" and "humanitarian" interventions could be justified.[16]

The discourse of human rights does evoke an evaluative approach towards one's own and other societies, according to pre-established common standards. In practice, however, it is the so called developed – and western – part of the world that denounces, intervenes and restitutes people's rights in the "underdeveloped and poor" parts of the world. Beyond the context of development discourse and its marketization of human rights, the debate over the justice of human rights should focus on how a discourse that raises claims to universality can persistently give rise to unilateral condemnations and interventions.

It has been my argument in this book that the search for such universal mutual understanding and agreement is not only possible, due to the normative condition of human interdependency, but that, in the age of globalization, it is also the requirement of social inclusion and self-understanding. The argument that antidevelopmentists raise against human rights as an "abuse of power" (Esteva 1996), may be the right conclusion but it is, nevertheless, for the wrong reasons.

The possibility of a comprehensive agreement on human rights as it stands now is submitted to the principles of national sovereignty and individual freedom. The idea of human rights intends to maximize the autonomy of the state vis-à-vis other states and its own citizens. It does not question the liberal principle of freedom on which the role and interplay of these actors is legitimized. Hence agreement on human rights, similar to the process of establishing national liberal constitutions, can be reached without a meaningful inclusion of the other, without the questioning and understanding of each other's world views and ways of life.

The purpose of the law, enacted as in a national constitution or intended as in the international bill of human rights, is to protect all against each other so that everyone can, as much as possible, freely pursue their preferences, both collectively and individually. The consequence of this process is that stronger social actors will inevitably have the upper hand, if not always in determining the *content* of the law but certainly in *interpreting* its meaning and most definitely in *applying* such interpretation. When agreement is restricted to the requirement of minimum and not maximum mutual understanding, addressing freedom and autonomy as individual possibilities – outside processes of mutual understanding – such agreement, as we have seen earlier, is at the mercy of asymmetrical power structures and antagonistic power relations. Human rights conceived on these liberal terms can easily become abusive.

Neither the antidevelopment critique of human rights nor development's argument for human rights and the absolute value of every human being address the foundational principles of the human rights discourse. Neither can for this reason explain nor understand international and multicultural relations within a symmetric power structure and cooperative power relations. The symmetry of power is found at the level of mutual understanding and it is here alone – in the

---

16   See Esteva (1996), Tasco´N and Ife (2008) and Hehir (2010).

search for *substantial* agreement fulfilled through a pre-validated *procedural* agreement – that norms and regulations like the bill of human rights can represent everyone's agreement on what would be the best course of action for everyone. The bill itself, as it stands now, is too "thick" to claim a procedural status and too "thin" to represent a substantial multilateral agreement.

If the abuse of power is to be overcome, substantial and thus meaningful agreement is to be achieved. Such effort *presupposes* a fundamental revision of the liberal claim to individual autonomy and national sovereignty and *requires* awareness of each other's irreplaceable value in validating decisions or *awareness* of our unconditional friendship. At the same time, it requires fostering acquaintance with people's particularities, caring for the decisions that each makes, listening, giving and demanding reasons for how people everywhere treat each other, that is, actively *fostering* global friendship through dialogue. The result of this process may be a bill of human rights. However, because it would have been the result of a search for mutual understanding, it will be more substantial and, therefore, more critical of cultural particularities that it may simply tolerate (or neglect) nowadays in the name of individual and collective autonomy. Far from a unilateral imposition, this critical approach will be the result of everyone's advancement in self-understanding.

Traditionally, respect to human rights has not required knowledge of the other's values and truth claims, concern for the reasons a society has to act in one way or another. Such respect has meant, in the best case, securing to peoples and nations the possibility of each making its own decisions while allowing others to do the same. No mutual understanding and agreement beyond this has been thought possible, necessary or desirable. Respect to human rights, because it requires so little in terms of self-sacrifice and is meant to maximize individual freedom, is turned, moreover, into a *duty* for every individual and collectivity.

In the discourse of human rights, the duty to respect other people's rights is derived from the condition of a common humanity and the fact of diversity. Diversity is a given fact of our lives and should be respected for the sake of our "humanity". Humanity is the capacity to choose freely and it is, therefore, the cause of individual and cultural diversity. As the choices of the other have just to be protected, regardless of their content, with the only mandate that they respect everyone else's freedom of choice, friendship is neither recognized as the prerequisite nor required as the means for such mutual respect.

While the duty to respect the other's rights asks us only to accept him as he is, friendship demands questioning one another's choices, asking about their content and continuously reviewing and transforming one's options in interaction with the other. The duty to respect does not say *why* we should do so and whether and how we have to change our own actions and behavior. Friendship evolves around the unconditional recognition that the choices and claims of the other *can* be validated. This recognition demands, in its turn, that everyone be actively engaged in the validation of individual and collective choices.

Although friendship is built on the unconditional recognition of the equal possibility of validation of the others' claims, this is an equality that requires active involvement and participation. It asks us to care for what the other does, for *how* he is asserting his capacities, because this *how* is affecting, at every moment, how we understand and fulfill our own capacity. What the other does cannot be *a priori* validated simply because it does not affect the exercise or fulfillment of our capacity, that is, what we *do*. At the level of *understanding* what these capacities are, there is no such privileged sphere of safety. The other's actions, once revealed to us, irreversibly determine how we understand and define ourselves. In a globalized world, where everyone's actions have become visible, mutual affection is global. We may choose in this case to foster relations of global friendship or choose to let our mutual affections be guided by the socially prevailing patterns of recognition.

Respect to universal human rights does not in itself require knowledge of the other's choices. Because these choices apparently do not affect our own and their value remains redeemable only for the performer, there is no basis for such demand. The assertion of the equal status of people's diverse choices that human rights proclaim implies, for this reason, the opposite of what the equality in friendship entails. Equality in the first case means equal freedom *from* each other, freedom from having to question or to answer to the diversity of actions and life styles. In the second it takes us to an active questioning of the ways we affect and ought to be affecting each other.

The fundamental question that the supporters of human rights ignore or prefer not to ask is why should a diversity that does not say anything to us and about us be preserved? The prevailing assumption is that the proclamation of these rights stands for universal equality – in which absence mutual respect among societies could not be. Nothing, however, is more distant from mutual respect and from the possibility of such respect than claiming the absolute and thus independent value of human diversity. One cannot help wondering, respect for what, when we do not care to know and do not find value in understanding anything about each other's choices? The assertion of an equality that is self-sufficient, that does not foresee a reason to go beyond itself and ask about the particularities of the other, cannot promote respect for the other.

We cannot respect those options which we do not *hope* to understand. We can only respect that which, although we may still not know and may never come to know, we have the always present hope of understanding. The hope, moreover, that as we understand, our self-understanding expands and our choices gain in meaning and value. Respect cannot be imposed as a duty, it can only come with familiarity with the other and towards those who enrich our lives. This is a familiarity that is not abandoned at the hands of the unknown future but is nurtured through commitment with the ever present promise of understanding that the other entails. When equality is asserted and the hope of mutual understanding is simultaneously and systematically denied, branded as naïve and as a practical impossibility, the relationship that results thereof is not of mutual respect but of fear of someone's power.

If the Universal Declaration of Human Rights was to be defined by a community of friends, it would be the result of an ongoing dialogue over the content of all peoples' traditions. The initial awareness of the possibility of mutual understanding would take the parties into questioning the value of each other's actual expressions. In this process some expressions will be agreed to be more conducive to everyone's self-expression than others. Because the Declaration, similar to modern law, only addresses the limits and the borders of legitimate action, it cannot tell people anything meaningful about their actions, no matter how well-established and multilaterally agreed it may be. It does not say whether what people are allowed to keep doing is better than what they are required to compromise or in what *particular ways* their so called legitimate choices speak to or contribute and hinder someone else's choice – which value, likewise, has not been understood and respect to which is, for this reason, the demand and imposition of arbitrary power.

If the Declaration was the result of friendship and dialogue between the peoples and nations of the world, it would be more coherent with what it proposes to achieve. Not only would it foster but also represent the actualization of relations of mutual respect. Validation through dialogue implies the recognition that everyone has something fundamentally valuable to say about another's choices. Although in dialogue one's choices are never preserved, the other does not represent a threat but the means of furthering self-understanding. As long as there is someone who is not convinced of the value of a particular choice and asks for reasons, the meaning and the value of individual and collective choice will be reviewed and patterns of thought and action gradually transformed.

As we seek to regulate international and multicultural relations on the basis of mutual respect, a goal that almost everyone can agree as being valuable, it is important to ask how each party justifies or values this goal. When someone's reasons alone prevail in this process, like the value of liberal Western individualism, mutual respect is hampered. This is not so because everyone's reasons were not equally validated in the process of interpreting this goal but because the process or procedure itself that has led to and which these dominant and partial reasons continuously re-validate cannot lead to mutual respect. Mutual respect, although a universally agreed goal, when carried outside dialogue is abidance to the reasons that the stronger party originally had to uphold such goal. Outside dialogue, the unquestioned and ignored but nevertheless present and diverse reasons of the weaker party to uphold to the same goal are reduced to fear. In the absence of more "honorable" reasons, respect is nothing but fear of the stronger.

Currently, the universality of human rights is justified and valued on the following terms:

> What persuades us to describe as reasonable the large range of very different
> doctrines that we find in the world is the reasonableness of the people who

hold them. It would be disingenuous to pretend that we account those doctrines reasonable because they have passed a test of 'reason' that we have devised independently and in ignorance of the doctrines that people actually hold. (Jones 2001: 31)

Human rights concern is "with people who hold doctrines, rather than with the doctrines that they hold" (Jones 2001: 33). It claims to respect people's diversity by presenting itself as a minimum regulation that tells them "how they ought to relate to one another as people with different beliefs" (Jones 2001: 34). Its task is not to judge the merit of each one of people's beliefs and values and "declare which doctrine is true and which is false" (Jones 2001: 37).

Nonetheless, how can it be argued that there is a way of respecting people without a concern or care for trying to understand what they do and who they are? And although we may accept the possibility of the other's reasonableness, how can we sustain it without being actively engaged in investigating the reasonability of their choices? What is the relevance and protection that such uncaring respect can offer to one's own life and to that of others?

Human Rights, Community Rights and Friendship

Antidevelopmentists are precise in identifying this and other incoherence in the human rights discourse that development sustains. They say that such norms and regulations are necessarily the reflection of a specific doctrine, that they cannot place themselves beyond every other doctrine, pretending to be free of content or substance. Human rights are seen as the imposition of one's way of life over others', a means of repressing people's diversity and the inalienable right of the community to decide about its own future. Mutual respect, they claim, cannot be found in the regulation of global relations but within local, caring communities. It is only inside their own communities that people can be truly valued and thus respected. If mutual respect is what development project truly stands for then, instead of imposing the right to development, it should allow each community to decide about its own way of life, free from external predicaments, regulations and "humanitarian" or global market interventions.[17]

Although the discourse of human rights, differently than what it intends, does not embody nor foster equal respect to the diversity of communities and to people's freedom and dignity, the defense of the community life according to the antidevelopmentist's standards of autonomy does not present us with a different alternative either. Both raise the same truth claims and their disagreements, more than on the content of their claims and values, is a conflict between power representations. But as we have extensively discussed here, if this is a conflict of

---

17   See Galeano (1997), Esteva and Prakash (1998), Escobar (2009), Porto-Gonçalves (2009) and Gudynas (2009).

power then there is no need for argumentation or justifications of any sort. There is only direct confrontation in the practical grounds of power struggle.

Evidently, however, this is a discussion over the truth of the claims that each side raises, that is, over the alternatives that do more justice to what peoples and communities are or that better corresponds to peoples' condition and contingent realities. The debate on development, on universal human rights and on the rights of the community are meant to present us with different understandings of our personal and collective reality and tell us how we ought to be relating with one another in order to get closer to that which we already look for in our daily interactions. The apparently divergent arguments that each side holds unto address, nevertheless, the same human condition and the same aspirations. Fear of death determines individual and community decisions, consolidating norms, regulations and social arrangements whereby the other is kept away, as much as possible, from interfering with or threatening one's survival. Because the debate does not question the truth claims that each side raises, it remains restricted to discussing only different alternatives to a similarly and poorly conceived humanity. Alternatives built on the same assumptions, no matter how divergent in strategies, struggle towards a common end and one does not represent, therefore, a social alternative in relation to the other.

From the perspective of human unity – peoples' equality and interdependence in the search for self-understanding – the universal dialogue that this unity or search calls for and the original pact of friendship that is implied and ever renewed in dialogue, the development debate depicts the structure of human relations in a fragmented and dirempted manner. But even if we are not to bring an external argument to the debate, such as the human condition of unity, I have shown that the debate abounds with internal inconsistencies. The last and overarching inconsistency being both sides claim for mutual respect. When people's condition has been *indirectly* reduced to that of self-preservation, even when respect seems to be in place it is instrumental, that is, for the value that the other contingently represents to one's survival. In this case a more coherent approach for both sides would not be demanding respect to the other's rights and autonomy but fostering each side's practical means of survival.

The defense of human rights as an assertion of the other's unconditional value *a priori* to one's *search* for value, a search that can only be validated in the actual struggle for recognition, is a inconsistent and hypocritical discourse. It expresses a pre-conceived disrespect to the contributions that the other can make to one's values and understanding. Diversity asserted simply as a fact of life, without knowledge of cause, reflects and re-enforces the understanding of the other and his values as a constant threat to one's values. As such, the discourse of human rights resembles more that of a fearful people who is trying to preserve their symbolic and physical self. Attachment to a pre-established self and fear of diversity take us to hide behind the shadows of our human rights, refusing to ask about the other's way of life and re-thinking one's own truths, because these are *already* valuable. Together with liberal individualism and the modern differentiation of the private and public spheres, human rights constitutes the compromising effort of modern men to keep his dear known self while letting others keep theirs.

On the other hand, those who defend the community and denounce the hypocrisy of relating such notion with the respect of people's diversity take advantage of the underlying fear of those who welcome diversity in ignorance, to demand the re-arrangement of community life according to its own values and criteria. Antidevelopmentists argument for the autonomy of the community intends, just like development's defense of individual rights, to preserve the community from the challenges of interaction. In their discourse only the members of the community can partake in the identity building process. The value of external participation is not recognized or at least it should not be a fundamental component in the shaping of one's identity.

But if the overarching goal is the preservation of people's ways of life and not the understanding of their meaning and value, which would have to include and respond to any other that raises question against a particular way of life, it would also be justifiable that each people pursue their survival through any available means – the means themselves not being given to critique and validation. In this process the one with more effective means will certainly impose himself over others. Because antidevelopmentists justify the autonomy of the community in these terms, there is really no way of maintaining such autonomy if the other is in practice more effective in the use of his tools of survival.

By overlooking the reasons why autonomy should be respected, antidevelopmentists leave autonomy at the hands of factors that are alien to its requirements. What could limit the indiscriminate use of one's resources is the fear of the other's retaliation and some instinctive compassion. These could actually work as strong motivators for "listening" to the other's demand and under such circumstances, the more antidevelopmentists were willing to threat the oppressor or ask for compassion, the more effectively they could support community's right to self-determination.

In practice, however, this has not been the social trend. The physical power of some nations has disproportionately outgrown that of others and fear and compassion become increasingly irrelevant in deterring the struggle for self-preservation. As society accumulates more and more effective means of survival, what also implies more means of destruction, its fear from the other decreases. It decreases along with its compassion that is turned into fury towards those who dare to challenge its strength. If communities do not agree to live according to the so-called "civilized norms of a global society" it is increasingly less likely that they would be allowed to keep their autonomy. The tendency, as we already witness, is for more tolerant discourses, like that of human rights, to be gradually overtaken by less tolerant social forces, resulting, for instance, in the "marketization" of human rights, the *duty* to respect these rights and increased unilateral interventions.

But although some are apparently succeeded more than others in surviving and preserving their autonomy, because human survival is a function of self-understanding, this privilege is misguiding. Although antidevelopmentists cannot coherently sustain and demand respect for people's diversity, development project is not more successful either in fostering survival and upholding the autonomy of its direct beneficiaries. For human beings survival is threatened by a hindered self-understanding. And given that self-understanding is a collective process, so is survival. If are to survive, we must increase each other's self-understanding, the conditions of which none of the sides in the development debate have questioned and sought to unravel.

Beyond the misguided alternatives and strategies offered by the development and the antidevelopment discourses, one must look at the condition of possibility of mutual respect to peoples' and communities' autonomy. Respect for human rights or for the rights of the community does not promote respect to peoples' autonomy and freedom because it overlooks the way human beings and communities are connected to one another. It ignores the original pact that makes not only the practice of autonomy but even the most basic struggle for survival a possibility.

Outside this pact, as the structure of their understanding and expression remains unacknowledged, our capacities do not thrive. The few capacities that have been pre-validated will constantly be re-enforced as the only possibility of action and self-understanding. To exercise our autonomy is to recover the original pact, to recognize our human unity, to remember our universal friendship at that moment when it still was without adjectives and attributes. When we recognize the other in that condition of interdependency that the search for the self asks for we are not forced to obey global or local rules in order to protect ourselves against each other. Our autonomy or freedom – and not simply our physical and symbolic survival – is no longer a possession that has to be protected from the other, imposing on us the duty to respect each other's borders. Freedom is exercised *with* the other. It is the gift of the other's friendship.

The community is indeed, as antidevelopmentists argue, the place where true friendship and mutual respect can flourish. The community cannot, however, seek self-definition first with itself and then with the others. It cannot look for the local as a prerequisite to engage with the global. This does not mean that the global is the prerequisite for engaging with the local either. The home of friendship is the *communitarian relation with the universal other*. It is the non-contingent reality of human relations that should determine engagement in community life and guide the relations between communities. In other words, both global and local relations have to be built on normative claims, claims that can be multilaterally validated. In this sense, it is not a physical community that is the locus of friendship but what community life evokes: care and the search for mutual understanding.

Care for each other's well-being and the effort to understand each other's reasons are principles of action that arise from an understanding of human unity or our original friendship. Local communities can express care and foster mutual understanding as long as they are aware that the original search of its members for self-understanding and recognition – or identity and belonging – can only be fulfilled with the other in his universality and not in his particularities alone. These principles of action can be present in global relations as they can be absent from community life. If a community recognizes the condition of possibility of care and understanding, thus nurturing the capacities of its members, it cannot exclude any other from its care under the pretext of him or her being an outsider.[18] If such exclusions happen, the care that the community offers is conditioned to its requirements of self-preservation, motivated simply by its fear of death.

What the proponents of community self-determination forget is that only a care that is unrestricted, that stems from universal friendship nurtures a meaningful community life, that is, fosters collective and personal self-understanding. Such community, as it welcomes its members in their strangeness – for they are not being welcomed simply in their common beliefs but also in their disagreements, in what they differ and can thus meaningfully offer to each other's understanding – has a global scope. The ideal of friendship requires, therefore, relations that are more global and formal than the ones antidevelopmentists stand for and, in their institutionalization, they are more communitarian and substantial than the global relations developmentists promote. What is missing in the global and local relations that each side advocates is a relationship where

> We ought to renounce trying to know those to whom we are linked by something essential; I mean, we ought to welcome them in the relation with the unknown where they welcome us, as well, in our distance. Friendship, that relation without dependence, without episode and yet into which enters all the simplicity of life, passes by way of the recognition of the common strangeness that does not allow us to speak of our friends, but only to speak to them; it does not allow us to make them the theme of conversations (or of articles), but is the movement of the understanding in which, speaking to us, they keep, even in moments of the greatest familiarity, their infinite distance, that fundamental separation on the basis of which that which separates becomes relation. (Maurice Blanchot, *L'Amitié* in Derrida 1988: 644)

Friendship finds expression in dialogue, the principle of action and the procedure that institutionalizes global and local relations of mutual respect. It is only in dialogical relations that peoples' capacity for understanding and expressing their uniqueness and diversity can be respected. In dialogue the original friendship or commitment with the search for understanding is freed from particular loyalties and interests and from the fear of death.

The choice that is available to us, therefore, is not between global relations regulated by a bill of human rights or local and self-sufficient relations built on the claim to community's self-determination. These apparently diverse choices present us, as we have seen, with the same and in the long run self-defeating alternative: collective survival. The real alternatives are between global and local relations of non-interference that ask *only* for obedience to the law – a law that is

---

18   Gelder's interview with Malidoma Somé from the Dagara tribe in Burkina Faso is very illustrative of this argument. See Gelder (1993).

"respected" under the threat to one's survival and self-preservation – and global and local relations of dialogue, which imply and foster relations of friendship and mutual care. This second option promotes self-understanding and allows for collective survival. The first does not foster self-understanding and can barely guarantee survival. The path that we choose is what will determine our collective development or our collective underdevelopment.

Chapter 8
Development as the Collective Search for Truth

Development is the process of self-understanding that results from the recognition of human unity and is expressed in the practice of dialogue. Friendship, in its turn, is the unconditional need for recognition that unites people in their inalienable search for understanding. Recognizing unconditional friendship or human unity is deciding to actively engage in relations of mutual care and friendship, that is, in dialogue and to promote one's own and others' development.

Since there is no global community of friends or relations among nations and countries regulated by the principle of human unity and dialogue, there is no nation and society in the world today that can be called developed. What we have is an underdeveloped globalized society that ignores its unity and its fundamental friendship and thus engages in a struggle for mutual independence, either through self-sufficiency or through domination.

On the other hand, however, to the extent that relations of universal friendship are real in some contexts, collective development or self-understanding is, at least locally, taking place. But far from determining a pattern of self-sufficiency, such relations point to a development process that unfolds as participation in these local and relatively small communities increases. Development reaches its summit as *all* the peoples of the world actually partake in the open and multileveled process of dialogue in search for truth and understanding.

Freedom for None or for All

The sides in the development debate have justified their discourses in terms of the absolute value of freedom and the ensuing need for mutual respect. Freedom has been the end in the name of which development programs and strategies have been established throughout the world and also the reason why these same programs have been hardly criticized. However, whether claimed as an individual or as a collective endowment, freedom has meant the possibility to pursue one's own interests free from external – individual or collective – interference. Development and antidevelopment discourses, therefore, have supported their proposals and social critique on the same claims to freedom *from* another. Their disagreement over the sphere where such goal can and should be institutionalized reflects each side's assumptions on the inherent relation between truth and power.

The development discourse raises claims, among other things, to the universal validity of global poverty and human rationality. On these claims mainly, it justifies its worldwide economic, technologic and political interventions, that is, the practical power of development. Antidevelopmentists question this unity between power and truth by challenging the truth of development's claims. Their challenge, however, does not go far enough; it does not expect an answer or justification from the contested – due perhaps to sheer hopelessness as they witness the ongoing history of Western's violence and irresponsiveness. The critics of development rule out, in the name of irreconcilable interests, the possibility of universal redemption. They reduce universal truth claims to power claims and inadvertently abandon their own truth claims at the hands of (superior) power.

Initially challenging development's truths from the perspective of silenced and inferiorized claims, the possibility of validating these claims or mutual understanding is soon renounced when antidevelopmentists practical proposal is restricted to demanding from the Western developed nations a politics of self-contention or non-interference in the decisions of autochthones communities. I say inadvertently because with this proposal, that is, by not justifying communities' claims against Western values and truths and whereby not demanding any substantial changes in the beliefs and patterns of thought of the developed world – other than in that aspect in which these beliefs *practically* affect others – they *indirectly* reduce the rich and diverse claims of the historically oppressed to the same negative freedom uphold by developmentists. Negative freedom, in its turn, implies the removal of one's claims from the arena of validation to the arena of power relations and power struggles. But if therein lies the possibility of reclaiming communities' freedom, the future of the peoples of the world looks at best grim.

Positive freedom, understood as people's fulfillment of their diverse capacities, signifies asking about the meaning, that is, about the possible social value of peoples' claims. In a globalized world, freedom is asking about the *global* value of each personal and collective claim. While negative individual freedom, better described as an individual (or collective) *belonging*, needs to be constantly guarded against the other, positive freedom as understanding and realization, on the other hand, requires placing one's claims in relation to another's claims. It requires active inquiry into the claims that legitimize global and local relations. Positive freedom is asking about the practical and normative value of these claims, about their truth and justice, even though they may be simply proposed to authorize and legitimize local relations.

Although development discourse justifies freedom on the basis of what *could* be universally redeemable claims, the actualization of such freedom does not depend on the universal validation of scientific rationality, modern technology and the free market economy, to cite a few examples. People can freely pursue their interests as they are aided by these truths, even when they are unaware or unwilling to accept such benefit. These truths are universal because, when supported by and actualized within existing society's power structures – and not by each person's search for truth – they supposedly benefit in an equal manner everyone's freedom. The global *power* of development and modernization, committed as it is with these truths, claims that it is, consequently, not arbitrary. It is not a self-referential and self-sufficient force that acts according to its whim, irresponsive to the interests of those whose lives it affects, even though the universality of its truth claims has not and does not need to be *validated* by everyone.

The way to freedom in development discourse is well represented, for instance, by Adam Smith's thesis that in a free-market economy people can promote others' interests without active concern for these interests. That is, in a society thus organized, one would not need to know the interest of others nor judge its social value in order to be free. Accordingly, he would not need to justify or prove to other the social value of his own goals. The free-market economy itself is in charge of determining the value of everyone's choices:

> The butcher sells meat to the consumer, not because he intends to promote the consumer's welfare, but because he wants to make money. ... The consumer, in her turn, is not trying to promote the interests of the butcher or the baker or the brewer, but to pursue her own interest in buying meat or bread or beer. However, the butcher and the baker and the brewer benefit from the consumer's search for her own satisfaction. (Sen 2000: 256)

What is overseen, however, is the simple fact that people are not benefiting one another with the search *itself* for personal satisfaction. They are instead benefiting from the fact that at a particular moment their interests luckily and randomly did not clash. If the consumer had not had the money to pay the baker, for instance, both would still hold to their original interests but the satisfaction of one would have meant the deprivation of the other. Adam Smith was normatively and empirically wrong in proclaiming that a free-market economy, by allowing each to individually fulfill his interests, can guarantee the furthering of everyone's interests – nor can, as a matter of fact, social grouping according to pre-established interests promote such foreseen harmony.

Taking Adam Smith's predicament to the arena of international relations and multiculturalism, it becomes even harder to foresee how the universal truth that he claims can normatively or practically overcome social antagonisms and foster global order and harmony. As antidevelopmentists point out, free-market economy and scientific rationality could at best benefit only those whose interests fall within the limits of what these truths are meant to foster – although it has been my argument that not even these are achievable. In the case that communities have interests other than increasing the consumption and the accumulation of goods their freedom cannot be enhanced by these Western verities. Antidevelopmentists conclude that for this reason freedom could only be secured as communities free themselves from each other's truth claims and are able to materialize their own truths within and through communities' power structures.

The observation that Western's truths cannot justify its global power, given the multiplicity of available truths and interests, takes antidevelopmentists to conclude that the exercise of power should be confined to that particular realm within which the truth claims of power can be redeemed. Thus while development maintains that its truths are universal and its power justifiably global, antidevelopmentists argue that, if anything, it is power that gives the appearance of universality to truth claims and that the boundaries of development power should thus be redefined. But with this claim antidevelopmentists are indirectly placing the uncontestable power of development inside an autonomous category within which power becomes capable of assuming its own characteristics, without regards for peoples' claims and interests. If no truth can be universally validated, the task of recovering parallel and so far inferiorized claims becomes the function of how inherently self-restraining superior power is and how effectively local power can be organized to face external powerful influences.

Development and antidevelopment discourses approach the relation between truth and power from opposite perspectives, defining the actualization of freedom within local and collective or global and individual spheres of organization and action. But eventually because the truths of modern development assert their value *a priori* and regardless to an actual validation and, on the other hand, because the truth claims of local communities are to be redeemed with members only, freedom as the final goal of both discourses is reduced to the possibilities that antagonist power relations can secure, preferably of course within the partial but still lawful limits of "mutual respect".

Freedom so understood, even though endorsed by prevailing social discourses and social institutions as a practical – powerful – possibility, suffers from a twofold problem that at the precise moment of its materialization undermines it at its core. First, regardless of how the individual or the community engage in patterns of recognition and behavior that foster cooperation and solidarity among the friends or among community members, when these are closed to those who do not share the same values and truths and do not actively welcome the participation of "outsiders" or "foreigners" in their decisions, the relations that they establish are not meaningful. These relations cannot tell individuals and communities what is the social value of their so called free choices. They serve only as a means for guaranteeing personal recognition and preserving established power representations; that is, preserving that particular established social order that pre-validates the value of one's choices.

Second, though it is assumed that each individual or community can pursue its own interests without external interference while a national or international "invisible hand" will protect all from what would be nowadays an all-annihilating clash of powers, freedom as an individual or collective *possession*, instrumentalizes mutual respect and puts it at the service of self-preservation. We may obviously choose a policy of good neighborhood and mutual respect but such harmonious co-existence, however, is not the inalienable condition of self-preservation. It is a conditional arrangement that can momentarily serve this purpose. At the event that survival or self-preservation are threatened by such arrangement, power will express itself maybe in a less tolerant, less respectful and bolder manner but not for this reason it would have become more selfish or less inclusive in its structure and purpose.

Freedom as the struggle for self-preservation not only hampers the fulfillment of interests other than survival but, paradoxically, threatens survival itself. When mutual recognition is restricted only to those who share the same symbols and built around them alone, our interests are reduced to the reproduction and preservation of these symbols. It is hard to say in this situation that anyone is understanding and fulfilling his own interests. Social symbols or the imperatives of social reproduction are rather determining our choices. The *struggle* for the preservation of social symbols or self-preservation, on the other hand, is an impossible struggle for human beings. It does not lead them into cooperation but into competition, mutual destruction and self-destruction.

Within socially determined horizons of normativity that legitimize the struggle for self-preservation – while simultaneously and necessarily denying the possibility of the collective redemption of personal value – feelings of humiliation and inferiorization are dealt with through confrontational and antagonistic power relations. Within this framework of social relations, experiences of disrespect are dealt with not as a rupture in original solidarity that would have to be collectively recovered but as stolen, and thus individually retrievable, personal value. Internally motivated social cooperation gives way to strategic and instrumental cooperation, determined by external forces and contingent circumstances. I have earlier discussed in this book why also for those social groups historically successful with the inferiorization of others, the result of the struggle for self-preservation are unquestioned patterns of social reproduction that grow in contradiction and self-destruction. The discrepancy between current levels of scientific knowledge, technological advancement and individual rights, on one hand, and environmental degradation and absolute economic and social deprivation, on the other, give empirical evidence to this normative claim. The increasingly unsustainable and intractable patterns of action and interaction that characterize life in Western, modern and developed societies, if of no other value, give at least witness to how the struggle for self-preservation, material and symbolic, leads to the eventual destruction of all.

Internally motivated cooperation is a function of non-contingent interdependencies. Although human beings depend equally on each other to survive or to preserve their lives, survival is contingent to self-understanding, that is, to knowledge and expression of one's capacities. It is also at this level of self-relation that human beings are non-contingently interdependent and cooperation unconditionally required. When the drive to survive is deviated from this condition it does not have any inherent reason to demand cooperation. Cooperation may still happen but not without the instrumentalization, and thus the oppression, of all participants therein.

In modern times self-relation is built on the principle of equality itself. This means that any social institution and social action must be legitimized on this principle.[1] Hence the legitimization of the struggle for self-preservation as a principle of social ordering depends on people's acceptance that equality is an integral part of this struggle, while practical inequalities would demand more of its institutionalization. The pursuit of equality carried within the arena of the struggle for self-preservation fosters, however, only negative freedom, which in terms of self-understanding, is no freedom at all. The individual or collective pursuit of such equality – the equal right to self-preservation – is an intrinsically contradictory, because asymmetrical, end and only possible if somehow everyone overlooks such contradiction.

A relation between individuals and communities that fosters freedom as self-understanding is not expressed through the current materialization of the modern principle of equality in the institutions of capitalism, democratic constitutional state or even in the international bill of human rights. This level of interaction materializes the principle of equality in dialogical relations of mutual care and friendship, which alone can express the non-contingent equality or equal interdependence of human beings. Freedom thus pursued liberates us not from the other but from the other as an antagonistic, opposing power. The chain that oppresses human beings – the chain of inequality – does not lie in their kindred nor in his actions, but in submission of the self to the mandates of the fear of death for the sake of a promised equality. A submission that does not take us anywhere, an aimless struggle doomed to fulfill nothing.

The Truth of Development Revisited

Social order built on intentional and non-instrumental cooperation or dialogue is the function of awareness of peoples' non-contingent interdependency. Such awareness implies that beyond and in spite the factual asymmetries of power in the struggle for survival and self-preservation, the means each person or community chooses to survive can be symmetrically validated. At this level of social interaction, the asymmetric preservation of the means of survival is submitted to the symmetric understanding of these means.

The establishment and consolidation of modern institutions that guarantee an equality of economic opportunities and equal political rights cannot overcome the antagonism of power relations and the inequality of power structures. Contrary to the modern way of thinking, equality or freedom from the oppression of

---

1   This is why, for instance, social critique in modernity is only sustainable (and understandable) in face of a reasonably argued inequality, either as a secondary or a constitutional aspect of society.

asymmetric power relations does not entail freedom *from* an oppressive other. Oppression is the unilateral assertion of knowledge, actions and skills, which results from commitment with the preservation of particular terms of validation, like the terms set by the capitalist division of labor, the demands of the market and the dominant political culture.

The historical expansion of human understanding has, as a matter of fact, gradually addressed social value in terms of an original symmetric relation of recognition. This learning milestone, however, has ironically been interpreted by the modern man as evidence that every social choice and action is equally valuable and that, therefore, the terms of a fair cooperation between social members requires only *impartial* institutions. They are impartial because purportedly neutral in the validation of individual and group choices – their validation supposedly going only as far as to authorize every choice that does not interfere with the choice of others. Their role is simply to secure to everyone and to every group of interest *equal access* to the pursuit of what modern societies consider autonomously and privately defined and validated notions of good. Furthermore, because these institutions are perceived as neutral in regards to the assent to preferred forms of life, the terms of validation and patterns of recognition that they materialize are rarely brought into public account as themselves being the source of inequality and oppression. The result is the perpetuation of self-enforced and unilaterally defined standards of validation and the continuation thereof of inequality and oppression.

Although the standards of validation of individual and group choices seem now, more than ever, released from the actuality of public relations, the assertion of equal value cannot overcome the requirement of universal validation nor foster freedom. Furthermore, those standards of validation and patterns of recognition that necessarily and practically prevail in society – popularized, among others, by the institutions of mass communication and education – justify themselves as the fair result of antagonistic power relations that are committed with the preservation of diverse and non-redeemable values.

If, in the age of universal equality, we are to recover and materialize our original equality in the validation of the standards of validation themselves, and thus redirect our current relations of strategic cooperation, exclusion and mutual oppression towards mutual liberation, social institutions are to be able to include the other in his universality, that is, in dialogue. This is why development should be redefined as the institutionalization of dialogue at every sphere of human action and at every level of interaction, local, global and regional. Implied in this argument is a conception of truth (or good) that loses its social value and is transformed into an arbitrary expression of power at the moment that it is captured as the truth – at the moment we refuse to submit our pre-understanding of reality to every other truth claim and, therefore, to review it.

When our understanding is rigidly institutionalized, when we do not welcome the interpellation of the universal other, we "free" ourselves from the other – because irresponsive to him – to submit to the fear of death. We hold to a reality that does not say who we are, what is our original social contribution or our contribution to the self-understanding of others and why, beyond our fear to lose it, survival is worth it. Truth is, nevertheless, sought to be preserved because its practical implications have been taken for the search itself. Attachment to the social recognition and practical power that the knowledge of truth favors hinders further understanding and replaces *the right to know with the right to be right*, that is, with the right to have power.

Social value and practical power are, normatively speaking, the function of universal validation or dialogue, even when, practically speaking, the majority participates only with its passive consent. In the absence of practical dialogue the understanding of value and the actions whereby legitimized seek only to preserve a particular self-relation. Understanding our personal and collective originality is restricted to the reproduction of pre-validated patterns of recognition. Dialogue, in its turn, tells us about our value as beings whose capacities are always transforming and improving, in the sense that they gradually promote the understanding and a diversified expression of the original capacities of an increasing number of people.

Dialogue further reveals the truth and it is at once the expression and the exercise of the power of truth. Differently from other powers or social institutions that are maintained as long as its "truths" can be preserved, the practical and normative demands of truth become the more compelling – more powerful – the more we question it in dialogue. As understanding expands, social institutions and practices change but, unlike the change imposed by power, this is not simply a reversal in power relations, unable to affect the antagonistic structure of these relations. Change motivated by the search for truth is a change in the structure of power, which accordingly grows in inclusiveness. Dialogical institutions do not seek to preserve themselves when the claims that they raise or the truth that they represent are not acceptable anymore. And the practical issue in this context is no longer is "not acceptable to whom" or whether the truth of one community can demand changes in the power of another.

Truth, as an understanding that claims to transcend the normative and contingent limitations of the individual knowing subject, looks for universal agreement. It looks for everyone's potential consent. Human beings are driven to know the universalizable and to act accordingly, that is, according to those precepts that can in principle have everyone's consent. Modern societies – perhaps because so many diverse and still purportedly equal truth claims meet and have to co-exist, raising constant and unprecedented doubts about one's knowledge of truth – have tried to find a way of reconciling the drive towards understanding with the new practical requirements of understanding. The ingenious path they found was to *assert* the validity of truth *a priori* to the other's consent. By doing so we have detached the truth from its constitutional structure – its universality – and are left with an empty image of truth that cannot fulfill our desire for truth. Such meager personal or collective truth gives witness more to our fears and limitations than to our capacity to transcend them.

By accepting that all truth claims are equally valid, modern social institutions are not attending to our desire to know the truth nor succeeding in preserving a pre-validated truth. They claim everyone's right to be different but foster social homogenization. Although diversity is a fact of human societies, a difference devoid of its universalizable potential, cannot say anything meaningful about and to those who are different.

Some would say that the assertion of people's equal right to be different stands at the crossroads between life and death. But let us not forget the search for universal validation that is implied in this assertion. The assumption that such assertion can be universally agreed on represents a struggle for survival that, in order to succeed, must be carried out in the sphere of validation and mutual understanding. For this reason, even if and after we agree that the sole purpose of mutual agreement ought to be the preservation of life, we are still left with the very practical question of why diversity should be preserved in the first place. Are the claims of diversity redeemable, fostering, in this way, increased understanding and expression of diversity?

The gradual encounter of different peoples and the demand for the recognition of the equal value of their diversity or their truths – even when this refers only to their "own" truth – represent a fundamental historical step in the organization of social life towards the understanding of the condition of possibility of diversity and towards the expression of this diversity. In other words, we can today, better than ever, act in conformity with the precepts of knowledge. Neither our drive to know the truth is threatened with the encounter of different truths nor the possibility of knowing the truth. What is challenged and will necessarily be transformed with this encounter is our knowledge of truth.

The encounter of different truth claims, which equal status has gradually been recognized, tells us of the unexplored possibilities of learning. It tells us that the search for universal consensus that many times we thought had been achieved was only a partial and temporary agreement. Our desire to know the truth may shun away from the new challenges and difficulties of knowing what is true and what is fair in face of a newly legitimatized and acknowledged diversity of truth claims. But these challenges also renew such desire as they imply the realization of the incompleteness and limitations of our knowledge. They do not necessarily talk about our incapacity to know the truth or the uselessness of our desire and previous endeavors. Instead, they offer to our ongoing search the possibility of further fulfillment.

The search for truth at any time and in any context has meant the search for that which is universal. The claim of truth few hundred or few thousand of years ago was not a claim different from what it is today. It was the search for a knowledge that would transcend social conventions and traditions and point to new possibilities of action and interaction, good and fair for everyone – everyone meaning of course only a few social groups.

With the expansion of our awareness of equality, the requirement of practical inclusion becomes a pressing imperative. This increased practical demand does not tell us, however, of a time when knowledge of truth was more readily accessible or of how the current indiscriminate and arbitrary assertion of equal value could alleviate its weight. The new demands tell us about the structural constraints to which agreement was submitted and about the ways agreement is still limited. The modern successful struggles for the recognition of the equal value of peoples' diversity should be approached as the possibility of coming to terms with the inclusion of every other person and community in the process of dialogue or in the search for universal agreement, an inclusion that the human drive to know has always implied.

Agreement and consensus are always a promising possibility when the truth is being sought. But agreement is an achievement always under siege when power alone is to keep it. This takes us again to the acknowledgment that even though agreement and consensus may be valued only for the purposes of survival, one's power to survive without truth – without redeemable claims – cannot secure anyone's survival, threatened as this power is in the imposed agreement that it requires.

On the other hand, not only do truth claims look for consensus but also consensus is only *normatively* sought on truth claims, on that which raises claim to universal redemption. Wherever there is consensus, even if practically maintained solely by power, those who maintain it are also upholding to supposedly redeemable claims. When claims, however, are to be practically validated only by some and do not welcome the interpellation of everyone else, they become in practice non-redeemable. In this case power can only keep the appearance of consensus (on truth) by concomitantly and *indirectly* legitimizing normative inequalities and reproducing practical exclusions.

No matter how much developmentists insist on the equality of individual rights and antidevelopmentists talk about the equality of community rights, as both deny the possibility of an all-inclusive search for truth, they are indirectly asserting and supporting inequality. By negating the value of diversity to the understanding of truth, and the imperative that every society is at the service of the human drive to know and understand, they are going against peoples' original equality and approaching it as a normative and practical impossibility.

Those who state that because of the evident diversity of claims a universal agreement is impossible are not concomitantly denying the value of agreement. By reducing and limiting the sphere of those who can participate in reaching agreement and consensus, they are replacing the value of the *search* for agreement with a partially pre-established agreement. They are transferring the universal consensus that people seek in their desire for knowledge to the hands of those who have the power to impose consensus either at the local or global level. When we assume that consensus cannot be reached on that which is the best course of action – that in principle a decision which is equally true and good for all human beings cannot be arrived at – we are simply legitimizing those agreements that are or can be maintained by the existing structure of power relations.

For the modern man, living in an age where, in the name of private freedom and equality, the search for consensus has to be kept within the limits of one's own house or one's community and cannot set loose from it, the easiest way to fulfill his drive to knowledge is to deny the equality of the other. It is to say, to go beyond formal equality, equality in front of the law, and establish patterns of recognition that classify and place the other in hierarchical categories that justify practical exclusions. Tacit agreements are established within social groups that other individuals and groups are not equal and that for this reason – and not due to modern requirements of private freedom and legal equality – their consent is not necessary.

Because the desire to know our true value cannot be overcome and it is actually actively cultivated by modern discourse and institutions and because the structure of this knowledge cannot be altered, every other who is recognized as an equal is consequently part of one's search for the truth. Caught in the dilemma of how to interact with another who is at the same time formally an equal but whose consent we are not supposed to look for and have, moreover, no institutional means to do so, as a society we are inclined to undertake two simultaneous and interrelated paths. In the relation between social groups formal equality is submitted to substantial inequality and in the relation between the members of the same group, or still in globalization processes led by the impersonal imperatives of social systems, formal equality is submitted to the reproduction of particular patterns and symbols of recognition.

I have discussed earlier this second process and want to briefly refer here to the first one. Instead of undertaking the more difficult and organizationally complex task of questioning social structures, so that these become more inclusive and dialogical, the modern man creates mental categories for inferiorizing the other. In the absence of sensible reasons and institutional means for including the other in our search for truth, we seek to convince ourselves that the other has no capacity to understand and validate our truth claims because he is either from another culture, from another race, gender, religion or social class, because he is physically and mentally inapt, or, in the case of our current discussion, because he is underdeveloped and ignorant.

Those few who dare to directly and actively question the other and look for his reasoned consent can be ridiculed and ostracized, labeled as naïve, not realistic or even dogmatic. The person who enrolls in actual dialogue could not be more in tune, however, with the spirit of the times. By engaging in dialogue and submitting his own truths to the judgment of his interlocutor he fully accepts the equality of his interlocutor, his capacity to understand another's claims, that is, to question and either accept or reject these claims. The truth that he holds may be rejected in this process but because he is looking for truth and he is aware of the condition of possibility of such knowledge, he is most ready and eager to engage therein. The irony, of course, is that such a person is commonly seen as unrealistically hopeful of the verity of his claims or too careless of others rights, while it could be reasonably argued that he is the only one who is willing to know and, for this reason, the only one who cares, a true friend indeed.

This is, in short, the dilemma of our age: having to assert each other's equal value without the normative and practical tools to validate such assertion – other than the symbolic currency that circulates mainly in the capitalist market place, in the mass media and in educational institutions. Once we are taken to accept our equality, our choices of interaction lie between forceful submission to arbitrary equality, in which case the different consensus that each power upholds finds it legitimate to indirectly inferiorize each other and, while questioning formal equality, engage eventually, if necessary, in direct violence; defining everyone's values according to the pre-validated standards of recognition of prevailing – and increasingly global – discourses and institutions, in which case nihilism and cynicism will set the emotional tone of human relations; or engaging with the other in a search for truth, through local associations and organizations that are committed to the principle and practice of universal dialogue and, simultaneously, through the systematization of discourses that legitimize and foster such local initiatives.

If the idea of development is to express the possibility of meaningful social change or an alternative power structure, it has to address both these processes and be itself redefined in terms of a collective search for truth – the only level of interaction where the exercise of power is symmetrically and universally inclusive. Through these processes the unsuccessful effort to secure a balance of powers through the promotion of freedom as freedom from one another, gives way to a non-instrumental cooperation between symmetric power relations, positive freedom and everyone's survival.

Development thus redefined overcomes the so claimed purpose of establishing a balance of power between nations, through the unquestionable assertion of equality and freedom and, at the same time, through the unilateral and arbitrary globalization of certain patterns and symbols of recognition. A symmetric and all-inclusive power structure is materialized as people acknowledge their original interdependency. And freedom is expressed as they include the universal other in their search for understanding and act according to a renewed understanding. Finally, as they recover their capacity to know, transcending the simple imitation of social symbols, survival becomes purposeful, that is, they understand the meaning and the value of the particular ways in which they survive.

Development as the collective search for truth does not allocate power at the hands of some. It gives power back to the collectivity of human beings. It determines, moreover, that survival and freedom are both threatened with the exclusion of any individual and collectivity from this search. We cannot satisfy the other's interest by trying to satisfy our own and neither can we satisfy our interests first. We can only benefit the other and ourselves by searching for truth. To the extent that our interests are at the service of this purpose, they can be fulfilled. When survival is sought for the sake of self-understanding, when we recognize that whereby we achieve the understanding and expression of our capacities, survival can be collectively achieved through non-strategic cooperation, without polarizing power relations. The only interest, moreover, that can be sought and can be fulfilled collectively through non-strategic cooperation is self-understanding. It is when people work together towards this goal that all their other needs and interests become mutually fulfilling, instead of mutually destructive. To put it in other words:

> People need not only to obtain things, they need above all the freedom to make things among which they can live, to give shape to them according to their own tastes, and to put them to use in caring for and about others. (Illich 1980: 11)

Or still:

> Unlike animals which depend for their sustenance on whatever the environment readily affords, human beings are impelled to express the immense capacities latent within them through productive work designed to meet their own needs and those of others. In acting thus they become participants at however modest a level, in the process of the advancement of civilization. They fulfill purposes that unite them with others. ... Every individual has the capacity to see himself in this light and it is to this inalienable capacity of the self that development strategy must appeal. (Baha'i International Community 1995: 20)

Development has not been approached and discussed as a process that must necessarily be collective, as a relationship of friendship and dialogue, where each part releases his or her capacities – and thus develop – by contributing to the understanding of others. To identify someone as developed has traditionally meant that someone else was (is) recognized as underdeveloped. The question thus has centered on who holds and who ought to hold the power to determine the patterns of mutual recognition. Should this process be carried by local communities alone? Could a minimum standard be established that every community and individual should recognize, regardless of how they would choose to define themselves? Who has the authority to recognize some as developed and others as underdeveloped?

Those who are aware of the absence of true – because agreed on – references in the institutionalization of such degrading representations have enlisted themselves to the cause of denouncing the illegitimacy of these Western patterns and standards of recognition and argued that the peoples of the world should recover their own local standards and symbols of recognition. On his side, very rarely has the white Western man tried to do the same. Rarely has he sought to justify and explain, in response to the standards of others, why he ought to be seen as developed in the first place. He has taken the truth of his life style for granted. His main concern has not been to argue and to validate with others the truth and the value of his choices but to determine instead effective strategies for implementing and imposing these choices on others.

What should also be questioned, nevertheless, beyond the authority of the Western man to set his life style as the criteria for evaluating the truth of every other way of life, is why the way development discourse recognizes others should be and is questioned, to begin with, and why, on the other hand, some have extended their way of life to others. Why not keep such supposed benefit to oneself alone?

The fact that we seek to undermine and invalidate the patterns of recognition of the "developed", points to the symmetric power that characterizes the relation of recognition. *Power, one can reasonably argue, is not with the "developed" but in the relation of recognition that he establishes with the "underdeveloped" and vice versa.* The way each defines the other – and not only the way each defines himself – is what determines the "developed" and the "underdeveloped" selves. By undermining the truth claims of the "developed", antidevelopmentists are not in this sense undermining his power. What the "developed" brings to the relation, his irreplaceability in the recognition that he gives to the other's truth, can never be invalidated, even though his particular recognition may and should be.

The actualization of this symmetric power in daily relations is a function of awareness of the equal irreplaceability that each person represents for every and any relation – and thus the power that every human relation has to affect everyone's self-relation, even of those who are not directly involved in a particular relation. This awareness takes us to dialogue with the other's relative truths, to look for a consensus on how can we, at each moment, best understand and express our capacities to promote the expression of everyone else's capacities.

Western patterns of recognition are questioned for defining people's capacity in a way that does not correspond with how they perceive themselves and expect to be recognized. But if the "underdeveloped" could simply recognize himself independently from the other's recognition and from how he, in his turn, recognizes the other, attributes like "underdeveloped", "poor", "lazy", "ignorant", would not provoke any action or reaction from him. But they do and they take people to write books, organize social movements, and mobilize against them because such attributes, although powerful, are unacceptable. They are unacceptable not simply because they are wrong – do not correspond with people's self-image and expectations – but also because they are true in their affect on people's self-relation, that is, because people know that in order to stand for their truths they must consider and address these other claims. Their value must be recovered with the same destructive other, whose degrading recognition is ultimately unacceptable.

This same search for the consent of the other is what propels development into global intentions and strategies. To say that this is simply due to capitalism's ambition and its need for a growing consumer market and cheap labor resources is to forget a more fundamental question. Why are people striving to accumulate and profit in the first place? Is this simply a quest for survival, for shelter and for food? What does economic growth represent to those who pursue and foster it? Obviously development is not just a matter of securing survival but also of improving, as developmentists would say, one's "quality of life". A life with "quality" implies a life that is worth living or living in such a way that one can understand the value of the specific way in which he is capable of surviving. If we look for economic growth it is because we understand that this option addresses and expresses what we consider valuable about ourselves, that is, through it we affirm the value of our existence. What is then implicit in the development practice is the same search that is inherent in antidevelopment discourse, the search for the value of the self, either collectively or individually defined.

The issue, however, is that development takes its life style for granted. It does not start with the assumption that a consensus is *possible* but that it *already* exists. Building on this assumption, the assent of the other is sought in a deviated manner. Instead of fulfilling the purpose of self-understanding, it is sought for the preservation of the self and its choices. As I have already explained, preservation without self-understanding is, nevertheless, an impossible goal. It takes us to reproduce patterns of thought and action that become increasingly incoherent and eventually self-destructive.

It seems clear that most of the times the other is included unintentionally in the ongoing re-definition of one's self, without participants, therefore, becoming aware of the symmetry of power that determines this and any other relation. If equality and freedom are to be fostered this involvement and participation are to become acknowledged and intentional for all sides. It is not enough to stand at the frontstep of our door, talking and sometimes shouting to an irresponsive other or, still, performing for an audience that is welcomed only in its silence.

Against how prevailing social institutions function, we should seize local spaces of existing community and friendship ties to engage in actual dialogue with the universal other. These local associations and initiatives with a present, immediate and most of the times known other, as long as dialogical, are an exercise in questioning and defining the *universal validity* of the claims that are raised therein. In this sense the claims that are locally raised are also open to everyone's interpellation, to everyone's questioning of the value of such claims. Because they represent active engagement in universal dialogue, such local associations raise the level of everyone's understanding and are the main instigator of social change. They recover the power of relations of recognition inside which *all* are equally irreplaceable, representing in their materialization the original pact of friendship that makes each one of us participants in everyone else's development.

As we reflect on the possibility of dialogue in the international arena, we are naturally led to question what would take stronger nations to cooperate with weaker ones in a non-strategic manner. What could possibly take them to dialogue and look for consensus with another who does not seem to pose any direct threat to their life and life style? As we have discussed, however, it is, first of all, a normative mistake to think that one's survival is secure when the other's search for self-understanding is being threatened. The only way to guarantee survival would be to constantly ask and be responsive to how we are affecting and determining each other's particular ways of surviving, that is, by fostering collective self-understanding.

From this perspective and precisely for this reason heavily armed nations could be defeated by weaker ones, which, as a matter of fact, they are. We do not lack in practical examples to denounce that the previous assumption expresses, moreover, an empirical mistake. Military and economically powerful nations are constantly threatened by weaker ones, no matter how great the gap that separates their power. The threat is not due to some special war strategies and secret techniques that the latter may have mastered – no matter how stronger nations try to ignore it and reduce the issue only to this confrontational level. The threat that the weaker represents is the result of the threat that he suffers, in turn, to his self-understanding or to the understanding of the value and meaning of the particular ways he has learned to survive. No survival is worthwhile if its value is not understood and until this understanding is cultivated, in a community of true friendship and dialogue, one has nothing valuable to lose. The threat that weaker countries represent to everyone's survival will remain as long as their agreement is not sought, not only in international but also in national affairs – in those decisions that traditionally have concerned national interests and national citizens alone.[2]

Military and economic power, no matter how impressive in their destructive strength, only poses a threat to one's life. But a life which value is not recognized can never really be threatened because it has nothing to lose by loosing itself. The struggle for a denied recognition and a damaged self-relation can only represent victory, even if in this process one has to give up his life.[3] Such loss, if and when it happens, would have been for the only purpose for which survival is worth. Survival for this reason cannot be directly under threat, unless self-understanding is. And when those who have been inferiorized in their self-relation assault the life of others, human unity is also made evident. The symmetry of power relations in the search for understanding, and the subordination of all other human dimensions to this search, is revealed in everyone's threatened existence.

When the understanding of one's capacities is at stake; when he is not welcomed as an equal; his contributions irrelevant; when he has to keep whatever he believes in and values only to himself; and when, furthermore, he has to confine his truths while others are allowed to carelessly expand their own; then the way to assert the value of the silenced truths – an assertion that in monologue will necessarily be arbitrary – is offering at their violated altar one's own life and that of those who (mistakenly) assumed their inferiority.

It is important to note that the source of feelings of humiliation and disrespect does not lie in the unequal distribution of material power. The fact that some people possess fewer means of destruction than others, less developed weapons and technology, does not constitute by itself a source of humiliation and a threat to collective survival. Nor for this reason would the leveling of material power do

---

2   For a similar approach to violence see Martinez Guzman (2002), Borradori (2003) and Habermas (2006).

3   For an analysis of terrorism as a rupture in human communication see Borradori (2003).

with such feelings. Furthermore, *offended equal* powers, if anything, are more, rather than less, likely to engage in direct conflict.[4] Nonetheless, regardless of their relative strength, humiliated people, that is, those who did not have their capacity to know the truth and the truth that they have known recognized, are always a threat to that power that has thus affected their self-relation. In short, no power is strong enough to protect itself against a denied self-understanding.

The answer to the other's threat does not rest in the struggle for survival, in strengthening one's security system or in weakening it in order to be less provocative of the other. The answer lies precisely in *how* we are going to decide what to do next. The decision of whether a nation should uphold to certain military or economic power, for instance, should be taken by the collectivity of communities and nations of the world and not only by the nation itself. It is a decision that has to be considered in terms of what it represents and says about a particular society, about its value and contribution to everyone else. Producing and possessing an atomic weapon, for instance, would be acceptable as a means of enhancing one's capacities if it equally contributed to the understanding and expression of the unique capacities of every other nation and community. If in actual dialogue it is decided that it does not, then this is a particular expression that has been invalidated, that has not been agreed as being true or fair and cannot, therefore, be carried out by any society. Until we do not ask how what we say and what we do affect each other's self-understanding and do not act in such a way as to enhance everyone's valuable contributions, there is no way that we can free ourselves from the other's threat and there is no measure that can possibly secure survival.

The implication of human interdependency or unity to the development debate is that it overcomes the question of whose patterns of recognition should eventually prevail and at what level of social interaction, that is, the question of self-preservation and survival. Because at the level of the mutual need for recognition, people are equally powerful, different patterns of recognition can and should be introduced when thinking about development. Different communities, recognizing their inalienable power and moving, therefore, beyond their fear of death, should be open and transparent in sharing with one another their patterns of recognition, how they view each other, how this view affects their own self-relation and how they aspire to be recognized.

The value of each other's symbols should be questioned not only in terms of what it says to those who hold them but also to those who do not have them and want to have them or still that completely reject them. One's symbols, like science and technology, religious beliefs, traditional practices, should be valued by every human being and social collectivity. By caring to interact and ask and answer each other what the expression of particular capacities means, by welcoming everyone as a promised friend, we are fostering everyone's understanding of their (true) self.

---

4   See, for instance, the analysis and data collected by Barash and Webel (2002).

Development as friendship or as the possibility of understanding and expressing one's capacities refers to a collective stage of learning and understanding that cannot be partial. In the age of universal equality and globalization, when validation has to be globally sought, there are no nation and people that can develop while others remain underdeveloped. We live in a time when only the recognition of every other as a friend can promote development. As we include in our search the other's truth claims and his inalienable friendship, fulfilling our longing for understanding, we develop, collectively, our original and diverse capacities.

As I have tried to show throughout this book, developmentists and anti-developmentists would do more justice to the individual and community freedom that they try to secure if, instead of looking for arguments and ways of imposing one's own patterns of recognition or overcoming those of others, they asked and suggested in which ways people from different communities, from the North and from the South, from the East and from the West, can contribute to each other's longing for knowledge. How can we ask each other about the truth of our understanding, the justice of our actions and the sincerity of our intentions? Or how can communities, with their diverse symbols and patterns of recognition, enrich one another's understanding of the meaning and value of their own capacities, as they validate together the collective local and global purposes that these capacities can serve, including the purpose of survival?

Bibliography

Apel, K.-O.a.W., G 1984. *Understanding and Explanation: A Transcendental-Pragmatic Perspective*.Cambridge, MA: MIT Press.

Appiah, K.A. 2005. *The Ethics of Identity*. Princeton and Oxford: Princeton University Press.

———. 2006. *Cosmopolitanism. Ethics in a World of Strangers*. Edited by H.L. Gates Jr. *Issues of Our Time*. New York: W.W. Norton & Company.

Aristotle. 1996. *The Nicomachean Ethics* Great Britain: Wordsworth Editions.

Baha'i International Community. 1995. *The Prosperity of Humankind*. Wilmette, IL: Baha'i Publishing Trust.

Barash, D. and Webel, C. 2002. *Peace and Conflict Studies*. 2nd edn. London: Sage.

Bauman, Z. 1999. *Modernity and the Holocaust*. fifth. Ithaca, New York: Cornell University Press.

Benhabib, S. 2006. *Another Cosmoplitanism*. Edited by R. Post and S. Scheffler. *The Berkeley Tanner Lectures*. Oxford: Oxford University Press.

Berman, J.B. 2006. The Ordeal of Modernity in an Age of Terror. *African Studies Review*, 49 (1), 1–14.

Bevir, M. 2001. Derrida and the Heidegger Controversy: Global Friendship Against Racism, in *Human Rights and Global Diversity*. Edited by S. Caney and P. Jones. London and Portland, OR: Frank Cass.

Bloom, A. 1988. *The Closing of the American Mind. How Higher Education has Failed Democracy and Impoverished the Souls of Today's Students*. New York: Simon & Schuster.

Boff, L. 1997. *Cry of the Earth, Cry of the Poor*. Translated by P. Berryman. New York: Orbis.

———. 2006. *Francis of Assisi. A Model for Human Liberation*. Translated by J.W. Diercksmeier. Second. Maryknoll, New York: Orbis Books.

Borradori, G., ed. 2003. *Philosophy in a Time of Terror. Dialogues with Jurgen Habermas and Jacques Derrida*. Chicago and London: The University of Chicago Press.

Calderisi, R. 2006. *The Trouble with Africa: Why Foreign Aid Isn't Working*. New Haven, CT and London: Yale University Press.

Caney, S. and Jones, P., eds. 2001. *Human Rights and Global Diversity*. London and Portland, OR: Frank Cass.

Chong, D.P.L. 2010. *Freedom from Poverty. NGOs and Human Rights Praxis.* Philadelphia: University of Pennsylvania Press.

Colussi, M. 2009. Lucha contra pobreza...o contra la injusticia? *Rebelión* [Online], (Abril). Available at: http://www.rebelion.org/noticia.php?id=83482.

Comaroff, J. and Comaroff, J. 2000. Millennial Capitalism: First Thoughts on a Second Coming. *Public Culture*, 12 (2), 291–343.

Derrida, J. 1988. The Politics of Friendship. *The Journal of Philosophy*, 85 (11), 632–44.

———. 2003. *On Cosmopolitanism and Forgiveness*. Translated by M. Dooley and M. Hughes. 2nd edn. London and New York: Routledge.

Edgerton, R.B. 1992. *Sick Societies. Challenging the Myth of Primitive Harmony.* New York: The Free Press.

Escobar, A. 1995. *Encountering Development. The Making and Unmaking of the Third World*. Edited by S.B. Ortner, N.B. Dirks and G. Eley. *Princeton Studies in Culture/Power/History*. Princeton, NJ: Princeton University Press.

———. 2009. Una minga para el desarrollo. *America Latina en Movimiento* [Online], 445 (Junio) 26–30. Available at: http://alainet.org/images/alai445w. pdf.

Esteva, G. 1996. Derechos Humanos Como Abuso de Poder. *La Opinion*, (Fev).

———. 2009. Más allá del desarollo: la buena vida. *America Latina en Movimiento* [Online], 445 (Junio) 1–5. Available at: http://alainet.org/images/alai445w. pdf.

Esteva, G. and Prakash, M. 1998. *Grassroots Postmodernism: Remaking the Soil of Cultures*. London: Zed Books.

Esteva, G. and Prakash, M.S. 1997. From Global Thinking to Local Thinking, in *The Post-Development Reader*. Edited by M. Rahnema and V. Bawtree. London: Zed Books.

Fenelon, J. and Hall, T.D. 2008. Revitalization and Indigenous Resistance to Globalization and Neoliberalism. *American Behavioral Scientist*, 51 (Aug), 1867–1901.

Foucault, M. 1980. *Power/Knowledge: Selected Interviews and Other Writings. .* New York: Pantheon Books.

Frankovitz, A. 2002. A Rights-Based Approach to Development and the Right to Development. *Human Rights in Development Yearbook*, 1–14.

Fraser, N. and Honneth, A. 2003. *Redistribution or Recognition? A Political-Philosophical Exchange*. London, New York: Verso.

Freire, P. 1999. *Pedagogy of the Oppressed*. Translated by M.B. Ramos. Twentieth. New York: The Continuum Publishing Company.

Galeano, E. 1997. To Be Like Them, in *The Post-Development Reader*. Edited by M. Rahnema. New York: Zed Books, 214–22.

Garcia, F. 1999. The Global Market and Human Rights: Trading Away the Human Rights Principle. *Brooklyn Journal of International Law*, (25), 51–97.

Gelder, S.V. 1993. Remembering our Purpose. The Teachings of Indigenous Cultures May Help Us Go Beyond Modernity. *In Context. A Quarterly of*

Humane Sustainable Culture [Online], (Winter). Available at: http://www. context.org/ICLIB/IC34/Some.htm.

Goldsmith, A. 2007. Is Governance Reform a Catalyst for Development? *Governance: An International Journal of Policy, Administration, and Institutions*, 20 (2), 165–86.

Gudynas, E. 2009. El día después del desarrollo. *America Latina en Movimiento* [Online], 445 (Junio) 31–3. Available at: http://alainet.org/images/alai445w. pdf.

Gutman, A. 2003. *Identity in Democracy*. Princeton, NJ: Princeton University Press.

Habermas, J. 1971. *Knowledge and Human Interests*. Translated by J.J. Shapiro. Boston, MA: Beacon Press.

———. 1984. *Reason and the Rationalization of Society (The Theory of Communicative Action, Vol. 1)*. Translated by T.M. Carthy. Boston, MA: Beacon Press.

———. 1990a. *Moral Consciousness and Communicative Action*. Cambridge, MA: MIT Press.

———. 1990b. *The Philosophical Discourse of Modernity*. Translated by F.G. Lawrence. Cambridge, MA: MIT Press.

———. 1998. *The Inclusion of the Other. Studies in Political Theory*. Cambridge, MA: MIT Press.

———. 2006. *The Divided West*. Translated by C. Cronin. Malden, MA: Polity Press.

Hafner-Burton, E. 2009. *Forced to Be Good: Why Trade Agreements Boost Human Rights*. Ithaca, NY: Cornell University Press.

Hamm, B.I. 2001. A Human Rights Approach to Development. *Human Rights Quarterly*, 23 (4), 1005–31.

Hartmann and Honneth, A. 2006. Paradoxes of Capitalism. *Constellations*, 13 (1), 41–58.

Heater, D. 1996. *World Citizenship and Government: Cosmopolitan Ideas in the History of Western Political Thought*. New York: St. Martin's Press.

Hehir, A. 2010. The Responsibility to Protect: 'Sound and Fury Signifying Nothing?' *International Relations*, 24 (2), 218–39.

Held, D. and Kaya, A., eds. 2007. *Global Inequality: Patterns and Explanations*. Cambridge, UK: Polity.

Honneth, A. 1992. Integrity and Disrespect: Principles of a Conception of Morality Based on the Theory of Recognition. *Political Theory*, 20 (2), 187–201.

———. 1995. *The Struggle for Recognition. The Moral Grammar of Social Conflicts*. Translated by J. Anderson. Cambridge, MA: The MIT Press.

Honneth, A. and Joas, H. 1988. *Social Action and Human Nature*. Translated by R. Meyer. Cambridge: Cambridge University Press.

Honneth, A., McCarthy, T., Offe, C., et al., eds. 1997. *Cultural-Political Interventions in the Unfinished Project of Enlightenment, Studies in Contemporary German Social Thought*. Cambridge, MA: MIT.

Horkheimer, M. and Adorno, T.W. 2000. *Dialetic of Enlightenment*. Translated by J. Cumming. New York: Continuum.

Howard, R.E. 1995. *Human Rights and the Search for Community*. Boulder, CO: Westerview Press.

Illich, I. 1980. *Tools for Conviviality*. New York: Harper Colophon Books.

———. 1992. Needs, in *The Development Dictionary. A Guide to Power as Knowledge*. Edited by W. Sachs. London: Zed Books.

Illich, I., Zola, I.K., McKnight, J., et al., eds. 2005. *Disabling Professions*. 5th edn. London: Marion Boyars Publishers.

Johan Galtung, J. 2004. Imagining Global Democracy. *Development and Change*, 35 (5), 1073–9.

Jones, P. 2001. Human Rights and Diverse Cultures: Continuity or Discontinuity?, in *Human Rights and Global Diversity*. Edited by S. Caney and P. Jones. London: Frank Cass.

Kohlberg, L. 1981. *The Philosophy of Moral Development: Moral Stages and the Idea of Justice (Essays on Moral Development, Volume 1)*. New York: Harper & Row.

Lambin, E. 2007. *The Middle Path, Avoiding Enviornmental Catastrophe*. Translated by M.B. DeBevoise. Chicago: The University of Chicago Press.

Maalouf, A. 2000. *Violence and the Need to Belong. In the Name of Identity*. Translated by B. Bray. New York: Penguin Books.

Makhijani, A. 2003. The Structure of Global Apartheid and the Struggle for Global Democracy. *Science for Democratic Action* [Online], 11 (3). Available at: <http://www.ieer.org/sdafiles/vol_11/11-3/apartheid.html>.

Martinez Guzman, V. 2002. *Filosofía Para Hacer las Paces*. Barcelona: Icaria.

McNeill, D. and StClair, A.L. 2009. *Global Poverty, Ethics and Human Rights. The Role of Multilateral Organizations*. New York: Routledge.

Mies, M. and Shiva, V. 1993. *Ecofeminism*. London, New York: Zed Books.

Nandy, A. 1997. Colonization of the Mind, in *The Post-Development Reader*. Edited by M. Rahnema and V. Bawtree. London, New York: Zed Books, 168–77.

Nietzsche, F.W. 1976. *On Truth and Lie in an Extra-Moral Sense*. Translated and edited by Walter Kaufmann. New York: Viking Penquin Inc.

Nowak, M. 2002. A Human Rights Approach to Poverty. *Human Rights in Development Yearbook*, 15–36.

Nussbaum, M.C. 1997. *Cultivating Humanity. A Classical Defense of Reform in Liberal Education*. Cambridge, MA: Harvard University Press.

———. 2001. *Women and Human Development. The Capabilities Approach*. Cambridge, UK: Cambridge University Press.

Nussbaum, M.C. and Cohen, J., eds. 1996. *For Love of Country*. Boston, MA: Beacon Press.

Onazi, O. 2009. Good Governance and the Marketization of Human Rights: A Critique of the Neoliberal Normative Approach. *Law, Social Justice & Global Development Journal (LGD)*. [Online], November (2). Available at: http://www.go.warwick.ac.uk/elj/lgd/2009_2/onazi.

Outhwaite, W., ed. 1996. *The Habermas Reader*. Cambridge, UK: Polity Press.

Peet, R. and Hartwick, E. 1999. *Theories of Development*. New York: The Guilford Press.

Pendell, E. 1951. *Population on the Loose*. New York: W. Funk.

Plato. 1956. The Works of Plato. New York: The Modern Library.

Pogge, T. 2008. *World Poverty and Human Rights*. Cambridge, UK and Malden, MA: Polity Press.

Porto-Gonçalves, C.W. 2009. Del desarrollo a la autonomía: la reinvención de los territorios. *America Latina en Movimiento* [Online], 445 (Junio). Available at: http://alainet.org/publica/445.phtml.

Quijano, A. 2000. Coloniality of Power, Eurocentrism and Latin America. *Neplanta: Views from South*, 1 (3), 533–80.

Rahnema, M. 1992. Poverty, in *The Development Dictionary. A Guide to Knowledge as Power*. Edited by W. Sachs. London: Zed Books.

———. 1997. *The Post-Development Reader*. London, New York: Zed Books.

Roberts, J.T. and Hite, A., eds. 2000. *From Modernization to Globalization. Perspectives on Development and Social Change*. Oxford: Blackwell.

Rodriguez, H. 2004. A 'Long Walk to Freedom' and Democracy: Human Rights, Globalization, and Social Injustice. *Social Forces*, 83 (1), 391–412.

Sachs, J.D. 2005. *The End of Poverty. Economic Possibilities for Our Time*. New York: Penguin Books.

Sachs, W. 1993. Poverty – in need of a few distinctions. [Online]. Available at: http://www.context.org/ICLIB/IC34/Sachs.htm.

———. 1997. The Need for the Home Perspective, in *The Post-Development Reader*. Edited by M. Rahnema. New York, London: Zed Books, 290–300.

———. 2007. In My Own Words: Fair Future. *Resurgence* [Online], Nov/Dec. Available at: http://www.resurgence.org/magazine/article69-in-my-own-words-fair-future.html.

———, ed. 1992. *The Development Dictionary. A Guide to Knowledge as Power*. London: Zed Books.

Sahlins, M. 1986. The Original Affluent Society, in *The Post-Development Reader*. Edited by M. Rahnema. London, New York: Zed Books, 3–21.

Sandel, M.J. 2010. *Justice: What is the Right Thing to Do*. New York: Farrar, Straus and Giroux.

Sarkar, R. 2009. *International Development Law, Rule of Law, Human Rights and Global Finance*. Oxford: Oxford University Press.

Sen, A. 2000. *Development as Freedom*. New York: Anchor Books.

Singer, P. 2009. *The Life You Can Save. Acting Now to End World Poverty*. New York: Random House.

Tasco'N, S. and Ife, J. 2008. Human Rights and Critical Whiteness: Whose Humanity? *The International Journal of Human Rights*, 12 (3), 307–27.

Taylor, C. 1994. The Politics of Recognition, in *Multiculturalism*. Edited by A. Gutman. Princeton, NJ: Princeton University Press.

———. 1995. *The Ethics of Autenticity*. Canada: The Canadian Broadcasting Corporation.

———. 2000. *Sources of the Self. The Making of the Modern Identity*. Ninth. Cambridge, MA: Harvard University Press.

———. 2004. *Modern Social Imaginaries*. Durham, NC: Duke University Press.

———. 2007. *A Secular Age*. Cambridge, MA: Harvard University Press.

Tortosa, J.M. 2009. Maldesarrollo como Mal Vivir. *America Latina en Movimiento* [Online], 445 (Junio) 18–21. Available at: http://alainet.org/images/alai445w. pdf.

United Nations. 1951. *Measures for the Economic Development of Underdeveloped Countries*. New York: United Nations.

Uvin, P. 2004. *Human Rights and Development*. West Hartford, CT: Kumarian Press.

Visvanathan, S. 1991. Mrs. Brutland's Disenchanted Cosmos. *Alternatives*, 11 (1), 147–65.

Walzer, M. 2007. *Thinking Politically. Essays in Political Theory*. Edited by D. Miller. New Haven and London: Yale University Press.

Young, I. 2000. *Inclusion and Democracy*. Oxford: Oxford University Press.

Yunus, M. 2007. *Creating a World Without Poverty. Social Business and the Future of Capitalism*. New York: Public Affairs.

Index